Challenging Common Core Math Lessons

ADVANCED CURRICULUM FROM THE CENTER FOR GIFTED EDUCATION AT WILLIAM & MARY

Challenging Common Core Math Lessons

Activities and Extensions for Gifted and Advanced Learners in GRADE 6

JAMES M. MORONEY

William & Mary
School of Education
CENTER FOR GIFTED EDUCATION

P.O. Box 8795
Williamsburg, VA 23187

Edited by Lacy Compton

Cover design by Raquel Trevino and layout design by Allegra Denbo

ISBN-13: 978-1-61821-489-8

Prufrock Press Inc.
P.O. Box 8813
Waco, TX 76714-8813
Phone: (800) 998-2208
Fax: (800) 240-0333
http://www.prufrock.com

TABLE OF CONTENTS

INTRODUCTION

The Common Core State Standards (CCSS) for Mathematics are K–12 curriculum standards that describe the mathematics skills and concepts students need to develop for success in higher education and the 21st-century workplace. The CCSS for Mathematics consists of two parts:

- The Standards for Mathematical Content, which define what students should understand and be able to do in their study of mathematics. The content standards balance procedure and understanding.
- The Standards for Mathematical Practice, which describe ways to process and show proficiency when engaging with a mathematical concept.

With the adoption of the CCSS in nearly every state, gifted and advanced learners need opportunities to master grade-level standards and mathematical practices with greater depth, rigor, and understanding. This book is one of a series of books developed in conjunction with the Center for Gifted Education at William & Mary intended to give gifted and advanced learners additional practice and activities to master and engage with the CCSS for Mathematics. Each book in the series is organized by the content standards in one grade.

The lessons in this book cover grade 6 mathematics content. In grade 6, the standards are addressed in five domains:

- Ratios and Proportional Relationships,
- The Number System,
- Expressions and Equations,
- Geometry, and
- Statistics and Probability.

STANDARDS FOR MATHEMATICAL PRACTICE

To engage learners with the Standards for Mathematical Content, the CCSS describes the Standards for Mathematical Practice—ways to connect with the content standards at every grade level:

1. Make sense of problems and persevere in solving them.
2. Reason abstractly and quantitatively.
3. Construct viable arguments and critique the reasoning of others.
4. Model with mathematics.
5. Use appropriate tools strategically.

6. Attend to precision.
7. Look for and make use of structure.
8. Look for and express regularity in repeated reasoning.

Each lesson in this book identifies the mathematical practices by number. Activities and practice problems are structured to develop mathematical practices in learners. Teachers should be aware of the practices and look for opportunities to connect mathematical practices to content understanding in every lesson.

PURPOSE

The lessons in this book were written with the assumption that a teacher has already introduced a mathematical content standard through a primary curriculum source. Problem solving, practice problems, and activities enrich and extend current grade-level mathematics content rather than accelerate students to above-grade-level content. Each lesson is specific to a standard, usually only focusing on one or two content standards, and provides additional support and enrichment for gifted and advanced learners.

LESSON STRUCTURE

Each lesson follows a predictable structure. It begins by naming the focal standard(s)—what students should already know or to which they have been introduced. Next, the Standards for Mathematical Practice covered within the activities and problems are listed by number. The lesson includes an estimate for the time it might take to complete the lesson; however, this will vary by teacher and classroom. Key terms are listed, and are included based on when the terms are first introduced in the CCSS or are a prerequisite for understanding the activity or problems in a lesson. Teachers should be sure their students already have a working knowledge of these terms before beginning the lesson.

Every lesson includes a list of materials needed, including handouts. It is assumed students will have access to commonplace items such as pencils and paper, and the materials noted are those items that teachers will need to obtain/acquire in advance. The lesson objectives highlight what students will learn or be able to do as a result of completing the activities and problems.

All lessons include an opening activity to allow students to explore the concept (e.g., multiple representations, open-ended problems, observing number patterns). Each activity is followed by practice problems that challenge students (e.g., harder or less familiar numbers) and—more importantly—extend students' thinking beyond calculating an answer. The practice problems ask students to grapple with their understanding of the lesson concepts. The lessons conclude with an assessment practice that allows teachers to evaluate student learning. The practice problems were written to engage gifted and advanced learners in higher level thinking and deeper understanding of a mathematical concept. The Common Core Assessment Practice problems in this book were intentionally written for students to practice and prepare for on-level standardized test questions similar to CCSS-based grade-level assessments, given all students are required to take these types of assessments.

GROUPING OPTIONS

The lessons in this book can be used for whole-group, small-group, and individual instruction.

Whole-Group Instruction

Teachers can use this book in one academic year in conjunction with the primary curriculum in a gifted or advanced mathematics class. All students would complete each lesson after being introduced to a particular content standard. Teachers can integrate the lessons into the primary curriculum taught to a whole group and address higher order thinking questions through the lesson activity and practice problems.

Small-Group Instruction

Teachers can use this book to differentiate learning in any mathematics class by creating flexible student groups and giving students who need enrichment an opportunity for deeper understanding and engagement with a concept. Students can complete activities and practice at a self-guided pace with a partner or small group and engage in peer discussion, with or without directed supervision or intervention from the teacher.

Individual Instruction

The practice problems and assessment questions in each lesson are a good way to determine individual understanding of a certain mathematics concept on a deeper level. Nearly every practice problem emphasizes making sense of and communicating the process of problem solving and asks students to explain their thinking.

SECTION I

Ratios and Proportional Relationships

LESSON 1.1

Ratios and Proportions

Common Core State Standards

- 6RPA.1
- 6RPA.3.a

Mathematical Practices

- 1, 2, 3, 4, 5, 6, and 8

Estimated Time

- 60–90 minutes

Key Terms

- Ratios
- Proportion
- Bartering

Materials

- Lesson 1.1 Activity: A Bazaar Relationship of Ratios
- Lesson 1.1 Bazaar Ratio Table for Exchange Rates
- Lesson 1.1 Bazaar End-of-Day Graphing Worksheet
- Lesson 1.1 Practice: Using Ratios
- Lesson 1.1 Common Core Assessment Practice
- Trivial items to barter (materials will vary based on what is available)
- Paper, pencils, pens, tape, and other items needed for the shops
- Furniture for shops (e.g., tables, chairs)

Objectives

In this lesson, students will:

- recognize ratio relationships and ratio language,
- design tables of ratios to find missing or unknown values, and
- organize the relationship between ratio values in a coordinate plane.

Lesson 1.1 Activity: A Bazaar Relationship of Ratios

In this activity, students will work in pairs to put together a shop in a bazaar setting where bartering is the main form of transaction. Students will first debate the value of each object and then assign a value to each object. Students will have much more freedom in bartering if they simply rank each of the items from least valuable to most valuable. For example, the students might agree that a pencil is worth more than a paper clip, but they might not all agree on how much more the pencil is worth. This will allow students to create a trading ratio between each of the objects and will allow groups to compare the ratios at the end of the activity to see how they might be similar or different. For a faster version of this activity, you can establish a common currency and value each of the items based on that currency.

Each pair of students will then design its shop around a trivial item (e.g., paper clips, paper, pencils). These can be brought from home or given to students by the teacher. Each group will have a different item. Students will design a series of ratio tables to represent potential transactions with their product and other products in the bazaar. For example, if Group A is trading cotton balls and one of the other products is staples, students in Group A will create a ratio table representing how many cotton balls they will need to give up to receive a sleeve of staples. They can then fill in the ratio table to represent hypothetical transactions for multiple sleeves. An example is shown in the chart below.

Cotton balls	5	10	15	20	25
Sleeve of staples	1	2	3	4	5

The student pairs should post these ratio tables on the outside of their shops as guidelines, but they should understand that in bartering the ratios might change a bit.

Students will then travel to the different shops in the bazaar and barter with the shop owners, completing a specified shopping list. After each transaction, both students will mark how much they paid and how much they received on Lesson 1.1 Bazaar Ratio Table for Exchange Rates worksheet. This will become the bartering ratio that can then be compared to the theoretical ratio tables that the students came up with while developing their shops. Students can use the bartering ratio to see if they got a better or worse deal than they had originally hoped for.

As a closure, on Lesson 1.1 Bazaar End-of-Day Graphing Worksheet, students will plot the ratio tables they created at the beginning of the lesson and the actual bartering ratio that they used during their time in the marketplace. Students will make at least four graphs that represent the relationship between objects. They should graph the actual ratio on the same graph as the preplanned ratio so they can visualize the difference in the two. Students should be asked to make a connection between the line on their graph and their ratio table (and ratios in general). Some students may even notice the difference in the steepness of the lines. As a class, compare the actual bartering ratios of each of the groups and discuss why the ratios are close (or not so close) to the other groups in the class.

NAME:________________________________ DATE:______________

LESSON 1.1 ACTIVITY

A Bazaar Relationship of Ratios

Directions: You and a partner are responsible for running a shop in an ancient bazaar where bartering is the main form of transaction. You will barter with the other shops in the bazaar using the agreed-upon exchange rates between objects.

Before You Begin

1. Establish an exchange rate between items. With your classmates, debate and rank the objects in the bazaar in order from least valuable to most valuable. Debate with your classmates how much of one object you would trade for an object of higher perceived value. Keep in mind the perceived value of each object in a classroom setting. For example, a sheet of paper may be considered more important than a paper clip, so you might establish an exchange rate of 10 paper clips for 1 sheet of paper (or a ratio of 10:1). This ratio might change a bit as the activity unfolds, but it will give you a good starting point when making your ratio tables.

2. Using Lesson 1.1 Bazaar Ratio Table for Exchange Rates, write the basic exchange rate for your product and other products in the market. You may use some of the ratios agreed upon during the discussion, or you might choose to alter them a bit as you see fit. Fill in the ratio table using the basic exchange rate and the equivalent exchange rates for trading multiple items. You might have something like 10 paper clips for 1 sheet of paper, so your next column in your ratio table will read 20 paper clips for 2 sheets of paper.

3. Make a shopping list of "needs" by looking at the other shops around the classroom and writing how much of each item you need. You will have to obtain these items during the bartering. Vary the amounts of the items for which you are shopping. For example, if you are shopping for two pencils, try to avoid also shopping for two erasers and two pens. Your shopping list might look like this:

Items Needed	1 piece of paper	2 erasers	20 pushpins	50 paper clips
Exchanged	1 sleeve of staples	1 sleeve of staples	1 sleeve of staples 2 erasers	5 sleeves of staples

Because you needed 20 pushpins, you exchanged one sleeve of staples and two erasers. You may not have had enough sleeves of staples to exchange for the pushpins, so you bartered with a value that was an equal amount.

During the Bartering Exchange

1. You and your partner will operate a shop in the bazaar. One of you will operate the shop, and the other will move between shops and do the bartering. You first priority as a barterer will be to obtain the "needs" from your shopping list. After about 5 minutes of bartering, you and your partner will switch roles, alternating at 5-minute intervals. Try to obtain as many items through bartering as possible. Remember that not all items will have an exact exchange rate. This is where bartering comes into play. In order to obtain the required items on your shopping list, you may need to barter with amounts that will not be an exact exchange. For example, if you need four sleeves of staples, you may need to barter with multiple items in order to complete the transaction. Look at the example below.

Items Needed	1 piece of paper	2 erasers	20 pushpins	50 paper clips
Exchanged	1 sleeve of staples	1 sleeve of staples	2 sleeves of staples	3 pieces of paper 4 erasers

If you need 50 paper clips to complete your shopping list, but are out of sleeves of staples, you might need to put together an equivalent offer, such as 3 pieces of paper and 4 erasers. Notice you have offered a combination of items that is of equal value to 5 sleeves of staples as shown in the chart on page 9. In some cases, you may need to offer more than the value of the item in order to make sure you complete your shopping list.

2. Move through the marketplace and barter with other shop owners by exchanging your items with them for other items. You may also barter with other shoppers instead of the merchants if you feel that you can get a better deal for an item you need. Write down the exchange ratio for each transaction that you make. You will need this exchange ratio when completing your end-of-day ratio tables.

3. At your shop, record all transactions you make on Lesson 1.1 Bazaar Ratio Table for Exchange Rates. You should vary the number of your item that you are exchanging. For example, if one of your customers barters for two of your item, no other customer may barter for two of your item.

After the Exchange

1. You must run an end-of-day operation to record all transactions throughout the day.

2. Complete Lesson 1.1 Bazaar End-of-Day Graphing Worksheet by plotting the ratio table that shows the relationship between your product and the other products

in the bazaar. You must graph both the original ratio tables you came up with at the beginning of the activity and the actual ratios you used while bartering. Graph each of the ratio tables and compare them.

3. With other groups, compare exchanges you may have made using other items besides paper clips to establish a common ratio between items based on that day's sales. For example, if one person exchanged 3 erasers for 6 pencils and another person exchanged 3 erasers for 4 pencils, the class may decide that the appropriate ratio is 3 erasers for 5 pencils.

4. Justify two of your transactions using ratio language. For example, 2 pencils were bartered for 8 erasers because every pencil is equivalent to 4 erasers. You could also say because an eraser is worth 2 paper clips and a ruler is worth 7 paper clips, we decided to exchange 4 erasers for 1 ruler to get as close to the ratio as possible while meeting the needs of our list.

Extend Your Thinking

1. Discuss with your partner the advantages and disadvantages of using a bartering system where buyers and sellers exchange items based on a ratio of perceived value. List two or three advantages and disadvantages on a piece of paper.

2. A new culture discovers your bazaar and wants to begin trading with an item you have never seen before. How could you and the other shopkeepers determine a fair way to set a value for the new item? You and the other shopkeepers can take turns bartering with the new item and establish a ratio between the new item and your product. How can you use ratios to establish a common value for the new item? Answer on a separate piece of paper.

3. Discuss what it may have been like when two unfamiliar cultures met for the first time (list examples on another piece of paper). How might these two cultures have determined the value of items and goods that were unfamiliar to them before they decided to start trading?

NAME:______________________________ DATE:______________

LESSON 1.1 ACTIVITY

Bazaar Ratio Table for Exchange Rates

Directions: As you and your classmates establish exchange rates, you and your partner should fill in the ratio table that represents the exchange ratio that you want between your item and all of the other items in the bazaar. Then fill in a similar table that shows the actual ratio between items that you traded while bartering.

Table 1: Exchange Ratio	
Your Item: ______________	
Bazaar item: ______________	
Your Item	**Bazaar Item**

Table 1: Actual Ratio	
Your Item: ______________	
Bazaar item: ______________	
Your Item	**Bazaar Item**

Table 2: Exchange Ratio	
Your Item: ______________	
Bazaar item: ______________	
Your Item	**Bazaar Item**

Table 2: Actual Ratio	
Your Item: ______________	
Bazaar item: ______________	
Your Item	**Bazaar Item**

Table 3: Exchange Ratio	
Your Item: ______	
Bazaar item: ______	
Your Item	**Bazaar Item**

Table 3: Actual Ratio	
Your Item: ______	
Bazaar item: ______	
Your Item	**Bazaar Item**

Table 4: Exchange Ratio	
Your Item: ______	
Bazaar item: ______	
Your Item	**Bazaar Item**

Table 4: Actual Ratio	
Your Item: ______	
Bazaar item: ______	
Your Item	**Bazaar Item**

Table 5: Exchange Ratio	
Your Item: ______________	
Bazaar item: ______________	
Your Item	**Bazaar Item**

Table 5: Actual Ratio	
Your Item: ______________	
Bazaar item: ______________	
Your Item	**Bazaar Item**

Table 6: Exchange Ratio	
Your Item: ______________	
Bazaar item: ______________	
Your Item	**Bazaar Item**

Table 6: Actual Ratio	
Your Item: ______________	
Bazaar item: ______________	
Your Item	**Bazaar Item**

NAME:____ DATE:______________

LESSON 1.1

Bazaar End-of-Day Graphing Worksheet

Directions: Now is the time to run an "end-of-day" closing for your time in the bazaar. On each graph below, plot the original ratio table that you established prior to beginning the bartering. Then, for the same item, plot the actual values that were exchanged during the bartering. Draw a line for each graph and compare the two. Do this for all of the different items for which you bartered during your day in the bazaar.

GRAPH 1

Exchange between ________________
and ________________ .

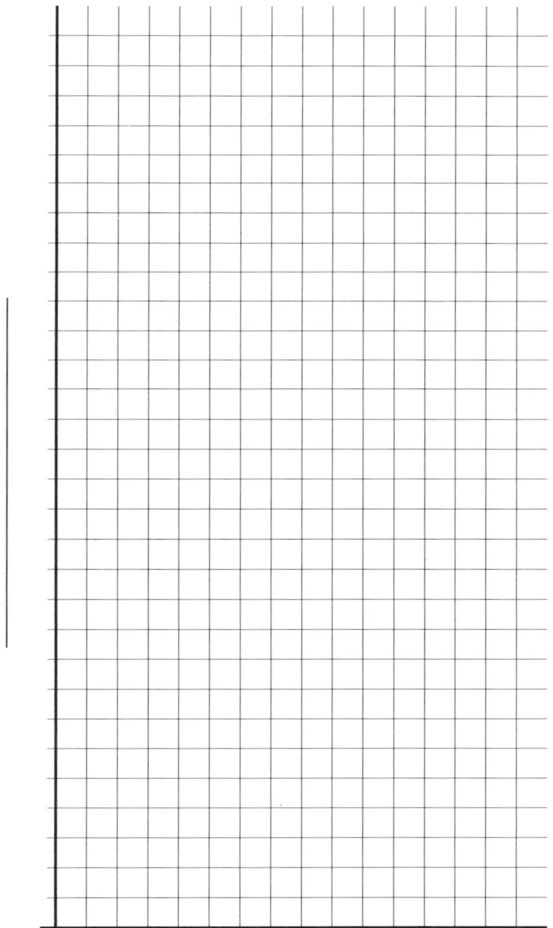

GRAPH 2

Exchange between ________________
and ________________ .

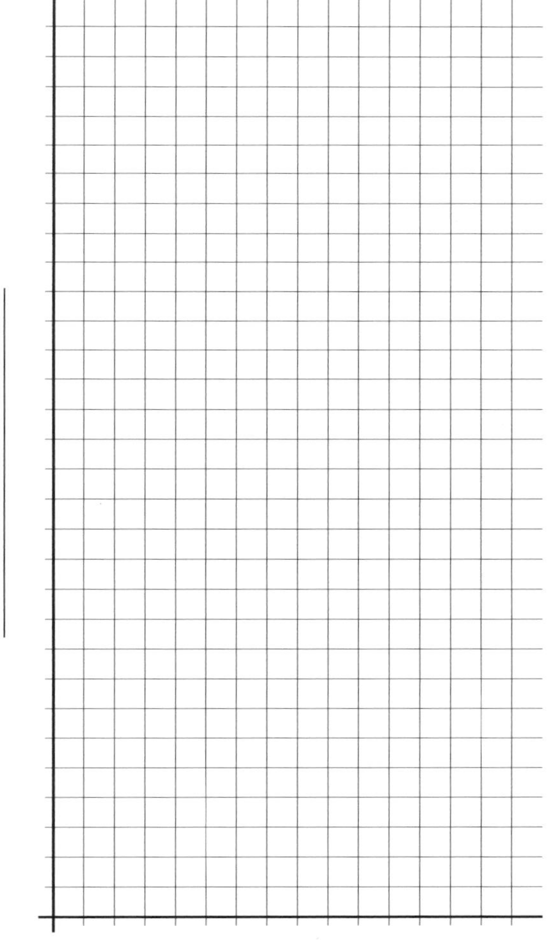

GRAPH 3

Exchange between ___________________
and ___________________ .

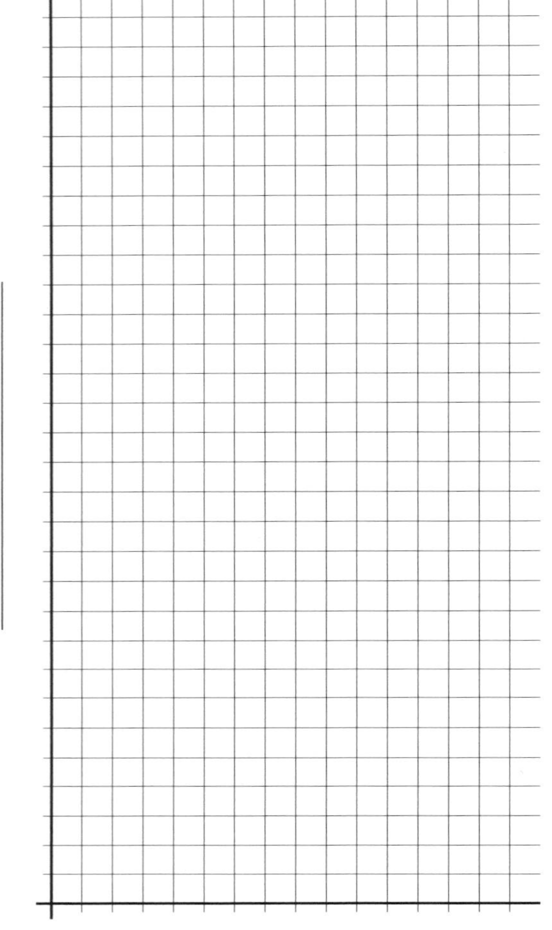

GRAPH 4

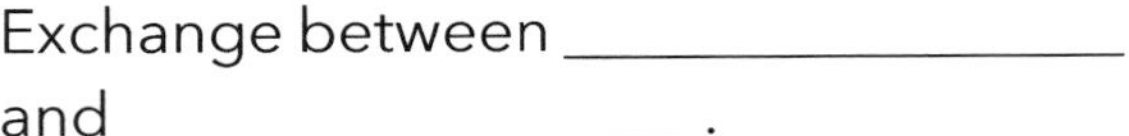

Exchange between ___________________
and ___________________ .

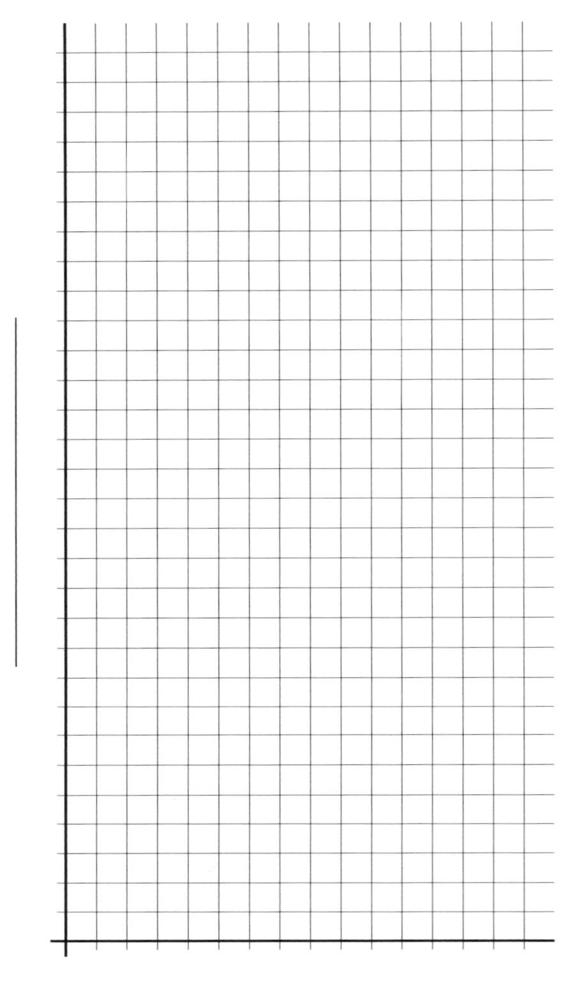

Ratios and Proportional Relationships

GRAPH 5

Exchange between ________________
and ________________ .

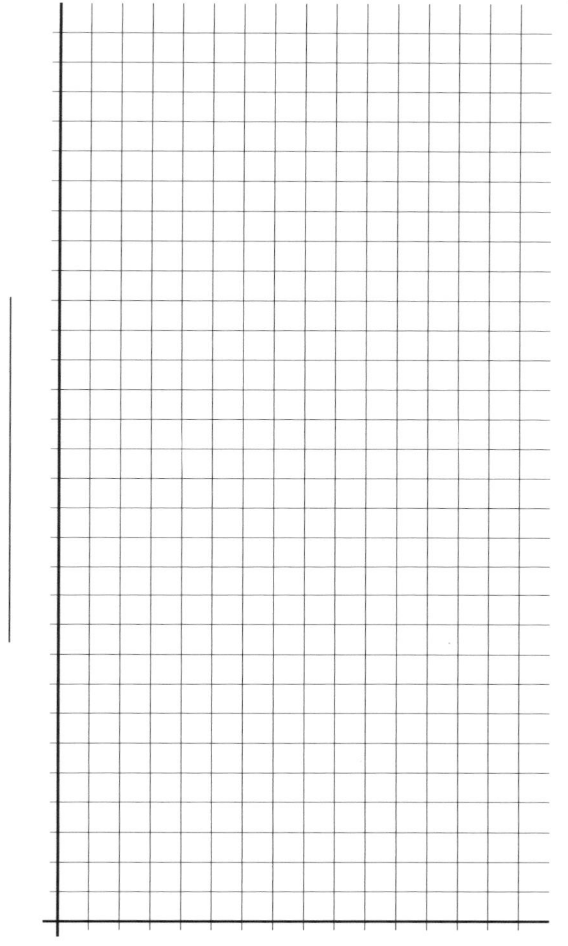

GRAPH 6

Exchange between ________________
and ________________ .

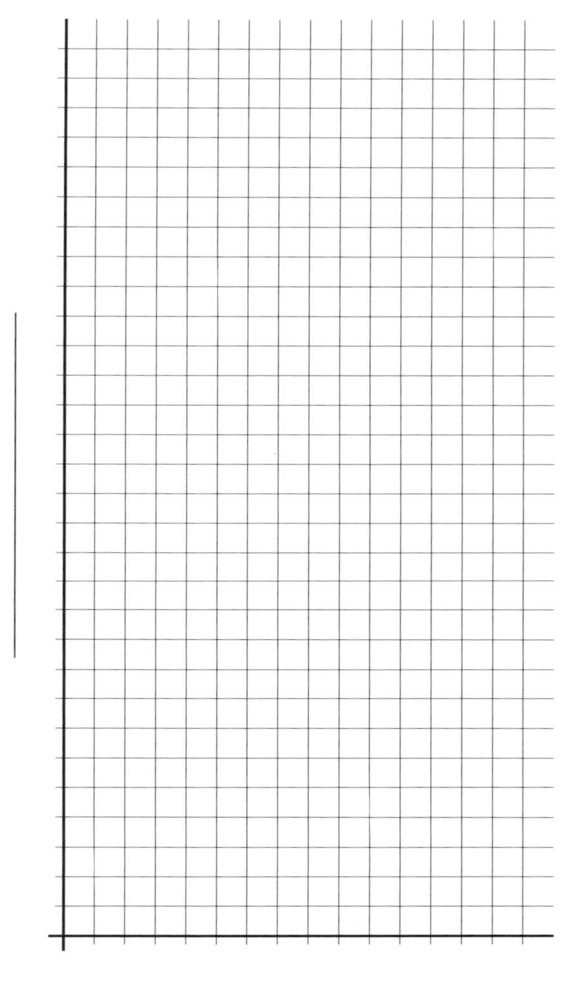

NAME:______________________________ DATE:______________

LESSON 1.1 PRACTICE
Using Ratios

Directions: Complete the problems below.

1. Jessica received a flyer for a new middle school that was opening in her neighborhood. The flyer stated that the ratio of teachers to students in all classrooms is 1:9. Jessica thought, "If there are four sixth-grade classrooms, there must be 32 students in the sixth grade."
   a. Is Jessica correct in her statement?

   b. Create a ratio table that proves your answer to Part A.

Classroom(s)				
Teachers				
Students				

   c. If you were Jessica's friend, how would you explain her mistake and teach her how to correct it?

   d. If the sixth-grade class has 4 classrooms, the seventh-grade class has 6 classrooms, and the eighth-grade class has 5 classrooms, how many total students are in the school? Show your calculations.

2. The ratio of women to total passengers on a ship is 3:8.
   a. If each part of the ratio represents 50 people, how many women are on board the ship and how many total passengers are on the ship?

b. Based on the numbers in Part A, how many total men are on the ship?

c. Write a simplified ratio for the number of women to men.

d. An additional 200 people board the ship. The ratio of the new passengers is 7 men for every 3 women. With the additional passengers included, what is the new ratio of men to women?

3. A local market encourages vendors to use bartering to buy and sell products. Monique talks with a man who is willing to exchange 25 beads for 6 of Monique's bracelets.

   a. If Monique gives him 18 bracelets, how many beads did she receive?

   b. The next vendor mentions to Monique that she usually only exchanges her ribbons for beads. "I exchange 2 ribbons for every 5 beads," she tells Monique. She notices that Monique has bracelets: "If you can figure out an exchange rate for ribbons and bracelets that is equivalent to what I exchange for beads, then we have a deal." What is an exchange ratio that Monique could offer to the ribbon vendor that would be fair?

   c. If Monique received 20 more ribbons than the number of bracelets that she gave to the vendor, how many ribbons did she receive? How many bracelets did she trade away? Use the exchange ratio from the answer to Part B.

Extend Your Thinking

1. Research the currency exchange between four different currencies from around the world (not the U.S. dollar). Make a basic exchange ratio table that compares the price of a U.S. dollar to each of the four different currencies.

2. Use the evidence in the ratio table to draw conclusions about the strength of the economy in each of the four countries.

NAME:______________________________ DATE:______________

LESSON 1.1

Common Core Assessment Practice

Directions: Complete the problems below.

1. Justin and his family visited the Audubon Zoo in New Orleans. After stopping by the monkey cages and the elephant cages, Justin realized there were 7 monkeys for every 2 elephants. If there were 10 more monkeys than elephants, how many elephants were at the zoo?
   a. 12
   b. 17
   c. 10
   d. 4

2. For a school field trip, the state law requires that there should be a ratio of 1 chaperone for every 5 students on the bus. There are currently 16 total people on the bus, with a ratio of 1 chaperone for every 3 students. How many more students can they add to the bus before going over the lawful limit?
   a. 4
   b. 5
   c. 9
   d. 15

3. A company currently has a ratio of 3 workstations for every section of the company. If the company has 5 sections and recently added 45 workstations, what is the new ratio of workstations to sections of the company?
   a. 5:1
   b. 9:1
   c. 12:1
   d. 15:1

4. The ratio of the distance traveled on a trip to the entire distance is 120:360. What is the ratio of the distance traveled to the distance remaining in the trip?
   a. 120:240
   b. 240:360
   c. 240:120
   d. 360:120

5. In a bazaar, 10 pounds of salt are worth 8 bolts of silk. If 2 bolts of silk are equal to 9 stacks of papyrus, how many pounds of salt are equal to 18 stacks of papyrus?
   a. 20
   b. 2
   c. 4
   d. 5

LESSON 1.2

Rate and Unit Rate

Common Core State Standards

- 6.RP.A.2
- 6.RP.A.3b

Mathematical Practices

- 1, 2, 3, 4, and 6

Estimated Time

- 60–90 minutes

Key Terms

- Unit rate
- Units
- Ratio

Materials

- Lesson 1.2 Activity: Rate Your Products
- Lesson 1.2 Unit Price Comparison
- Lesson 1.2 Advertisement Storyboard
- Lesson 1.2 Practice: Comparing Unit Price
- Lesson 1.2 Common Core Assessment Practice
- Technology or materials needed to develop an advertisement
- Various products for consideration by students

Objectives

In this lesson, students will:

- understand the concept of a unit rate, and
- solve unit rate problems, including unit price and constant speed.

Lesson 1.2 Activity: Rate Your Products

In this activity, students will work in groups to research three different brands of one type of edible grocery product (e.g., cereal, chips, yogurt, cheese). Students will use unit rate to make an advertisement highlighting the best buy and which reasons make their product of choice the best buy. Students should make their decision based not only on unit price but also on nutritional facts that may come into consideration. (The decision doesn't have to be strictly based on nutritional facts, but students may feel that it adds to their commercial.) Students should design their advertisement so that it compares the three products and attempts to sell one of the three products over the other two. Students should design their advertisement to compare the strengths and weaknesses of the products. Remind them that advertising for a specific product will usually focus on the strengths of the product that they are trying to sell and the weaknesses of the product(s) against which they are competing. Encourage students to use the product's unit rate to compare it with the other products. Students should try to show that their product offers more value for the cost than the other competing products using calculations of unit rate.

NAME:______________________ DATE:______________

LESSON 1.2 ACTIVITY
Rate Your Products

Directions: You are in charge of advertising for a product that is being sold at local grocery stores. You need to make an advertisement that shares the unit price of your item compared to other competitors selling similar items.

1. Begin by choosing three different brands of the same food item. For example, chips may be considered a food item, and Lays, Pringles, and Cheetos would be three different brands of chips.
2. Calculate the unit price of the three items. Use the Lesson 1.2 Unit Price Comparison handout to show your work and explain how you found the unit price for each item.
3. Your advertisement will advertise the item that has the cheapest unit price and is the best buy.
4. Compare the product that you want to sell to its competitors. In your advertisement, you should try to highlight the strengths of your product (in this case, its unit price) and point out the weaknesses of the other products, specifically how the unit price is higher than that of your product.
5. Create a storyboard for your advertisement. Use Lesson 1.2 Advertisement Storyboard handout to assist you.
6. Present your advertisement to the class. Be sure to explain how your group calculated the unit rate and decided which purchase is the best buy.

Extend Your Thinking

1. As each group is presenting, make an observation about each group's best buy compared to the other products in that group. After all of the advertisements have been presented, discuss with a partner a pattern that you noticed among the "best buys." How can you and your partner hypothesize which products will be the best buys?

2. You are selected to appear on a food show at your local TV station. You must create a "recipe" composed of food items that were used in the activity and presented by you and your classmates. Although it may not be an actual recipe, try to think of products that might go well together in a dish. Be creative! Choose four products that were presented. Specify that the ratio of the products used in the dish needs to be 4:3:2:1. For example, if you want to make a four-layer dip, you would use 4 ounces of guacamole, 3 ounces of black beans, 2 ounces of corn, and 1 ounce of sour cream to keep the ratio 4:3:2:1. Your teacher may assign a specific amount that your recipe needs to make. Calculate the unit price of one of your recipe items by taking into account how the ratios were used.

3. You are in charge of planning a grocery list for a month in your house. Reflect on the items that each of the groups presented during the activity. Choose three items. Think of how many of each of the items you might use throughout a month. For example, if one group presents on cereal, you might use three boxes of cereal in a month. After planning out a grocery list, calculate how much you would save total by choosing the better buys in each of the categories.

NAME:______________________________ DATE:______________

LESSON 1.2

Unit Price Comparison

Directions: Choose three items that fall into the same category in a grocery store. For example, you might select three different types of soda. Identify the product and its cost. Notice what weight or volume is used to measure the product and list the amount in the space provided. Then, calculate the unit price for each of the products to see which one is the better buy.

1. **Product 1:** ______________________________

Cost of this product: ______________

Product is measured in: ______________ (e.g., ounces, pounds, grams, liters)

The unit price is: ______________

2. **Product 2:** ______________________________

Cost of this product: ______________

Product is measured in: ______________ (e.g., ounces, pounds, grams, liters)

The unit price is: ______________

3. **Product 3:** ______________________________

Cost of this product: ______________

Product is measured in: ______________ (e.g., ounces, pounds, grams, liters)

The unit price is: ______________

4. How did you calculate the unit price of your products?

5. Is there another way you could have figured out the best buy without calculating the unit price?

NAME:______________________________ DATE:____________

LESSON 1.2

Advertisement Storyboard

Directions: Create an advertisement using unit prices that compares your product with two of its competitors. Advertise your product as the "best buy" by comparing it as the obvious choice over its competitors. Use mathematics as support to your argument.

1. In the boxes below, show the different unit prices as a comparison for each of the products. You may also brainstorm ways that your product is better than the other product (besides the price), so that you can use these in your advertisement.

Positive Qualities of the Best Buy	Negative Qualities of the Competitor

2. Use the squares below to brainstorm and roughly design your storyboard for your advertisement. The medium through which you present your advertisement is up to you.

NAME:______________________________ DATE:______________

LESSON 1.2 PRACTICE

Comparing Unit Price

Directions: Complete the problems below.

1. Bob's T-Shirt Outlet recently sold 50 T-shirts for $627.50.
   a. What is the unit price for one T-shirt at Bob's T-Shirt Outlet?

   b. If each T-shirt costs Bob's T-Shirt Outlet $5.35 to make, how much profit did the store make with its order of 50 shirts?

   c. If Bob's T-Shirt Outlet sells 250 shirts every week, how much money did the store make over a 3-week period? How much of that money was profit?

2. A competitor, Quality Shirts, opens down the street. It wants to sell better quality shirts for a cheaper price than Bob's T-Shirt Outlet. It costs the store $7.75 to make each shirt, and they sell each shirt for $11.90.
   a. How much profit does Quality Shirts make per shirt?

   b. How many shirts would Quality Shirts have to sell to earn more **profit** than Bob's T-Shirt Outlet?

c. Quality Shirts has to set aside $500 a week from its profits in order to stay open for business. This cost includes employee salaries, electricity bills, and building rent. Fahad, the owner of Quality Shirts, wants to know how many shirts he needs to sell in order to earn enough profit to put $1,000 in the bank each week. Considering the $500 overhead, how many shirts will he need to sell each week?

Extend Your Thinking

1. Choose a recipe from Allrecipes.com or another website of your choice. Determine the total cost of making the meal by using the prices for each of the ingredients in the recipe. Explain how to figure out the price per serving of the recipe based on the number of people it serves and the total cost to make the meal.

NAME:____________________ DATE:____________________

LESSON 1.2

Common Core Assessment Practice

Directions: Complete the problems below.

1. Diner Doughnuts sells a dozen doughnuts for \$3.96. Bargain Do-nuts sells 3 doughnuts for \$0.93. How much money would a customer save if he bought a dozen doughnuts from Bargain Do-nuts instead of Diner Doughnuts?
- **a.** \$0.15
- **b.** \$0.24
- **c.** \$0.28
- **d.** \$1.24

2. Ben has a 20-gallon tank in his SUV. Gopher Gas, which is located right near his house, sells gas for \$3.58 a gallon. Around the corner, Franklin Gas sells gas for \$3.61 a gallon. If Ben has to fill his tank twice a month, how much money will he save in a year by purchasing gas from Gopher Gas every time?
- **a.** \$12.24
- **b.** \$12.50
- **c.** \$14.20
- **d.** \$14.40

3. What is the unit price of T-shirts that cost \$48.60 for 3-dozen shirts?
- **a.** \$16.20
- **b.** \$1.62
- **c.** \$1.35
- **d.** \$1.12

4. Jordan's car gets 35 mpg on a 16-gallon tank of gas. If Jordan is taking a trip that is 1,425 miles long, how many times will he have to refill his tank before he reaches his destination, assuming that he begins the trip with a full tank of gas?
- **a.** 1
- **b.** 2
- **c.** 3
- **d.** 4

5. A sedan travels 516 miles on a 16-gallon tank of gas. An SUV hybrid travels 445 miles on a 14-gallon tank of gas. Which car is more gas efficient?
- **a.** Sedan
- **b.** SUV Hybrid

LESSON 1.3

Percent as a Rate

Common Core State Standards

- 6.RP.A.3c

Mathematical Practices

- 1, 2, 4, 6, and 8

Estimated Time

- 60–90 minutes

Key Terms

- Percent
- Rate

Materials

- Lesson 1.3 Activity: A Healthier Percent
- Lesson 1.3 Practice: Calculate the Percent
- Lesson 1.3 Common Core Assessment Practice
- Suggested websites (see description of activity)

Objectives

In this lesson, students will:

- find the percent of a quantity as a rate.

Lesson 1.3 Activity: A Healthier Percent

Students will begin planning for this lesson by cataloging the number of calories they eat per day over the course of a week or two and breaking them into five specific categories of a nutritional plan outlined by http://www.choosemyplate.gov: fruits, vegetables, grains, proteins, and dairy. Students will then calculate the percentage of the five food groups that they have in their typical diet (i.e., their best guess for the food they would normally eat in a day). After breaking down their diet into percentages, students will compare their diet to a recommended diet for students their age. In a discussion with the rest of the class, students will note discrepancies in their diet compared to the suggested diet and brainstorm foods they could substitute in order to make up the differences. In this way, students, with the help of their classmates, will create their own nutritional plan using percentages. Students will then map out their own food pyramid based on caloric breakdowns of the food they eat and their own percentage calculations.

You can download the necessary charts that you would need to complete this activity from http://www.choosemyplate.gov (see Food Tracker Handout, Calorie Calculations Worksheet, Food Pyramid Plan Handout, and Healthy Food Options Handout). The website has enough information on it for you to tailor this activity to your class. You can use conversions and more complicated percentages if you want to make the lesson more challenging. You can also simplify it for the sake of time by limiting the food groups recorded or simplifying the conversions/percentages. For example, you could make everything out of 2,000 calories and estimate calorie intakes to make the percentage calculations work more easily.

NAME:______________________________ DATE:______________

LESSON 1.3 ACTIVITY

A Healthier Percent

Directions: How healthy is your diet? In this activity, you are going to compare your current diet with that recommended by health and nutritional professionals. Then, after you have calculated the breakdown of your current calorie intake, you will make a food plan that falls in line with percentages recommended by doctors and nutritionists.

1. Over the course of 1–2 weeks, fill out the Food Tracker Handout by making a list of the current foods you eat, the number of calories (best estimate) of each food item consumed, and the category (fruits, vegetables, proteins, grains, and dairy) that the item falls under. Only list the foods that you would typically eat on a week-by-week basis. If you attend a birthday party and have cake, that would not necessarily fall under a normal food habit. Also, if you get a large bucket of popcorn at the movies one weekend, that doesn't need to be listed unless you go to the movies consistently week to week.

2. In class, using your Calorie Calculations Worksheet, total up the number of calories you eat in a week as well as the specific breakdown of calories per food group. Then, using your knowledge of calculating percent using rates, calculate the percentage of calories that are vegetables, fruits, proteins, grains, and dairy (show your work using rates).

3. Discuss with your class how your percentages compare with the percentages recommended by doctors and nutritionists. Where are the differences? What foods do you notice that might influence the percentages negatively or positively?

4. Create a food plan using the Food Pyramid Plan Handout. Calculate the total number of calories needed in each category based on the recommended amounts of each of the five food groups. Make a list of foods that you could add to your plan so that you meet the recommended percentages. Discuss with your class and teacher healthier calorie options to substitute for current foods on your list. Use the Healthy Food Options Handout to assist you in making your food plan.

5. Share your food plan with the class and discuss how you calculated your percentages and what food decisions you made based on the evidence and recommendations.

Extend Your Thinking

1. Discuss the foods on your Food Tracker Handout with your partner or group. Discuss which foods would fall under "good" foods and which could be labeled as "bad" foods. Calculate the percentage of foods that are "good" foods and the percentage of "bad" foods.

2. Compare your Food Tracker Handout with your Food Plan Handout. Make a note of the areas in which you made changes to your current diet. Calculate the percentage increase and percentage decrease of calories made to your current diet. For example, if you currently only eat 150 calories of vegetables each week, but you changed that to 450 calories each week in your Food Plan, you would calculate the percentage increase from 150 to 450 as a 200% increase in vegetable calories.

3. Using the percentages that you calculated in Extension 1, figure out how you would have to alter your diet so that the foods you eat would fall into the healthy category. Determine by how many calories in certain areas you need to increase or decrease your diet in order to maintain a healthy diet. Calculate that percent increase and decrease of these changes. Base your decisions on the percentage of carbohydrates, proteins, and fats that you should have in your diet on a daily basis.

NAME:________________________ DATE:____________

LESSON 1.3 PRACTICE

Calculate the Percent

Directions: Complete the problems below.

1. On a specialized food plan designed by her nutritionist, Maria noticed that 40% of her diet needed to be vegetables. Currently she is consuming 375 calories in vegetables per day on her 2,500-calorie diet.
   a. What is the current percentage of her diet that is made up of vegetables?

   b. How many more vegetable calories does she need to add to her diet to get to 40%?

   c. Maria decides to buy a bag of baby carrots to increase the vegetables in her diet. She reads that a serving of baby carrots is 40 calories. If she has $4\frac{1}{2}$ servings of carrots, what percentage of her additional vegetable calories (from Part B) does she consume?

2. A farmer is planting his crops at the beginning of spring. He wants to devote 24% of his acreage to green beans. His sets aside an additional 50% of his crops for corn.
   a. If the remaining acreage of his farm is for tomatoes, what percentage of his crops will be tomatoes?

   b. If the farmer owns 60 acres of land, how many acres are set aside for each crop?

   c. A late freeze kills a quarter of the corn that the farmer planted. How many acres of corn are remaining after the freeze?

d. The farmer makes $5,000 an acre for the green beans, $10,000 an acre for the corn, and $8,000 an acre for the tomatoes. What percentage of his total earnings comes from his tomato harvest? Assume that the number of acres of green beans and tomatoes comes from Part B and the number of acres of corn comes from Part C.

Extend Your Thinking

1. The next time you go to the grocery store, make a list of foods (no more than four) that you think have the best good-calorie per cost ratio. Determine the healthiest items that you can buy at the grocery for the cheapest price. For example, which foods give you the most amount of nutrition for the cheapest price?

NAME:________________________ DATE:____________

LESSON 1.3

Common Core Assessment Practice

Directions: Complete the problems below.

1. Benjamin purchased 150 of the 200 available chickens from the farm. What percentage of the chickens did he buy?
   a. 30%
   b. 60%
   c. 75%
   d. 85%

2. If Jody ordered 55% of the 400 bolts of fabric from her supplier, how many bolts of fabric did she order?
   a. 110
   b. 220
   c. 300
   d. 330

3. Miles had completed 25% of his race by 10 a.m. If he had already run 3 miles, how many miles did he have remaining?
   a. 4
   b. 8
   c. 9
   d. 12

4. Only 30% of a 20-gallon tank of water is filled. If a valve pumps water into the tank at 2 quarts every 15 minutes, how many hours will it take for the tank to fill completely?
   a. 7
   b. 10
   c. 14
   d. 28

5. A farmer receives $0.72 for every ear of corn that he harvests. His main crop comes from an acre of farmland just north of his house. If the farmer is able to harvest the entire acre, he gets 5,000 ears of corn. If he received $2,484 from his crop this year, what percentage of his crop did he harvest successfully?
   a. 35%
   b. 44%
   c. 60%
   d. 69%

LESSON 1.4

Converting Units

Common Core State Standards

- 6.RP.A.3d

Mathematical Practices

- 1, 2, 4, 6, 7, and 8

Estimated Time

- 60–90 minutes

Key Terms

- Units
- Measurement

Materials

- Lesson 1.4 Activity: Converting Units Taboo
- Lesson 1.4 Converting Units Taboo Cards
- Lesson 1.4 Converting Units Taboo Worksheet
- Lesson 1.4 Blank Taboo Cards
- Lesson 1.4 Practice: Converting Units
- Lesson 1.4 Common Core Assessment Practice

Objectives

In this lesson, students will:

- convert units using ratios.

Lesson 1.4 Activity: Converting Units Taboo

Students will begin this lesson by partnering up into pairs. Each team consisting of two students will be challenging another team to a game of Converting Units Taboo. Each team will receive a stack of Converting Units Taboo (CUT) Cards. One student will do calculations to give hints to his or her partner while the other student will use the hints to do his or her own calculations and make a guess at what value is on the card. Students will keep track of their calculations on the Converting Units Taboo Worksheet. On each card will be a given unit value and a unit that the students cannot use in their hints. For example, the card might read 96 inches, and the taboo unit might be feet. Students would have to give another hint besides "8 feet" to help their partner guess 96 inches. A student from the other team should be checking the person giving the hints to make sure he or she doesn't say the taboo word. After one team has gone through the cards, the other team will get its chance to give hints and guess. Both teams will get 5 minutes to go through as many cards as they can. The team that gets the most correct conversions wins the round.

If you want to focus on specific conversions, you can include the required word part of each card into the game. The required word forces the clue-giver to use that specific measurement in his or her hint. A card will look like this:

36 inches

Taboo Word:
Feet

Required Hint:
Yards

If you want the students to use the required word, students would have to use the measurement of yards when giving their hint.

LESSON 1.4 ACTIVITY

Converting Units Taboo

Directions: You and your partner are competing in a game of Converting Units Taboo (CUT) with another pair of students.

1. Shuffle your stack of CUT Cards.

2. The group with the oldest player goes first.

3. One student will then draw a CUT Card.

4. This student will try to get his or her partner to guess the value on the card by giving equivalent values without using the taboo unit. For example, the card might read 36 inches and the taboo unit might be feet. The student might give his or her partner this hint without using the taboo unit: "This value is equivalent to 1 yard, and you would probably use this unit to measure the length of a pencil." The student also could have said, "This unit of measurement can be converted into yards" or "This unit of measurement is found on a ruler." Be creative as you think of your clues.

5. If you were assigned to use the required word part of the card, the clue-giver has to incorporate that word or phrase into his or her hint in some way. For example, if the required word is yards, you must use the yards conversion in your hint.

6. Both the clue-giver and the guesser need to complete their Converting Units Taboo Worksheet where they show their conversion work using ratios. For example, the clue-giver receives a CUT Card that shows 36 inches but he or she cannot use the word feet. In the hint blank, the clue-giver will write yards, miles, or centimeters as possible units to use in his hint. The clue-giver will then make the conversions to find out how many yards, miles, or centimeters are equivalent to 36 inches.

   When the guesser receives the hint, he or she will write the possible units that the card might be. So in this case, the guesser might have guessed inches or feet depending on the clue (this can be changed as the clue-giver makes corrections based on incorrect guesses). For example, if the guesser receives the hint that this value will be equivalent to 1 yard, the guesser will then convert 1 yard into the units that he or she thinks is correct and proceed to guess that as the value on the card. If the guess is incorrect, the clue-giver can give the guesser more hints.

7. Groups will see how many cards they can guess correctly in 5 minutes. While one team is competing, the other team needs to be checking its math and guesses to make sure the team giving the clues and guessing is getting it correct.

8. Then the other group will take its turn to see if it can guess more.

Extend Your Thinking

1. Now that you have played the game, create your own taboo cards with unit values and taboo units that cannot be used in the conversion hints.

NAME:______________________________ DATE:______________

LESSON 1.4

Converting Units Taboo Cards

96 inches **Taboo Word:** Feet **Required Hint:** ________________	4 miles **Taboo Word:** Feet **Required Hint:** ________________	2 gallons **Taboo Word:** Quarts **Required Hint:** ________________
16 yards **Taboo Word:** Feet **Required Hint:** ________________	2 hours **Taboo Word:** Minutes **Required Hint:** ________________	8 weeks **Taboo Word:** Days **Required Hint:** ________________
5 liters **Taboo Word:** Milliliters **Required Hint:** ________________	8 meters **Taboo Word:** Centimeters **Required Hint:** ________________	9 kilometers **Taboo Word:** Meters **Required Hint:** ________________
15 milliliters **Taboo Word:** Liters **Required Hint:** ________________	24 inches **Taboo Word:** Feet **Required Hint:** ________________	0.5 miles **Taboo Word:** Feet **Required Hint:** ________________

NAME:______________________________ DATE:______________

LESSON 1.4

Converting Units Taboo Worksheet

Clue-Giver	Guesser
1. Value on card: ____________ Units to use in hint: ____________ Conversion work: ____________ = ____________ ____________ = ____________	**1.** Potential units: ____________ Conversion work (based on hint): ____________ = ____________ ____________ = ____________ Guess: ____________
2. Value on card: ____________ Units to use in hint: ____________ Conversion work: ____________ = ____________ ____________ = ____________	**2.** Potential units: ____________ Conversion work (based on hint): ____________ = ____________ ____________ = ____________ Guess: ____________
3. Value on card: ____________ Units to use in hint: ____________ Conversion work: ____________ = ____________ ____________ = ____________	**3.** Potential units: ____________ Conversion work (based on hint): ____________ = ____________ ____________ = ____________ Guess: ____________

NAME:______________________________ DATE:______________

LESSON 1.4

Blank Taboo Cards

________ (value, include units) **Taboo Word:** ______________	________ (value, include units) **Taboo Word:** ______________	________ (value, include units) **Taboo Word:** ______________
________ (value, include units) **Taboo Word:** ______________	________ (value, include units) **Taboo Word:** ______________	________ (value, include units) **Taboo Word:** ______________
________ (value, include units) **Taboo Word:** ______________	________ (value, include units) **Taboo Word:** ______________	________ (value, include units) **Taboo Word:** ______________
________ (value, include units) **Taboo Word:** ______________	________ (value, include units) **Taboo Word:** ______________	________ (value, include units) **Taboo Word:** ______________

NAME:______________________________ DATE:______________

LESSON 1.4 PRACTICE

Converting Units

Directions: Complete the problems below.

1. Joshua works at an aquarium store in his hometown. The manager asks him to empty and refill all of the display aquariums in the store. Joshua uses a 1-quart bucket to fill each aquarium.
   a. If each aquarium needs to have exactly 10 gallons of water, how many times will he need to fill his bucket to fill the aquarium?

   b. Joshua times himself. He realizes that he can fill the 1-quart bucket in 15 seconds. If there are 40 aquariums to be refilled, how many minutes will it take him to fill every display aquarium in the store?

   c. After Joshua has filled all of the aquariums, another employee puts the fish in the tanks. Joshua is in charge of getting the food together for the fish. Joshua knows that each fish in the tank gets 1 teaspoon of food per day. If Joshua uses 35 cups of food over a week, how many fish are there in the store?

2. A distance runner, Selene, is running across the country from Boston to San Francisco for charity. The distance from Boston to San Francisco is 3,100 miles.
   a. Selene runs exactly 200 miles a week. If she has already run for 10 weeks, how many days does she have left until she reaches San Francisco?

   b. Selene's best friend is the CEO of a major U.S. company. His company pledged to donate $0.01 for every foot that she ran. How much has she earned so far in the 10 weeks that she has run?

c. Selene limits herself to 10 hours of running per day. How fast is she running in miles per hour?

Extend Your Thinking

1. How fast do you travel on your way home from school? Make a note of the distance (in miles) from your school to your home and the time (in hours) that it takes you to get home. This number will probably be a decimal. Calculate the average miles per hour at which you travel during your drive. Then, convert your average speed into kilometers per hour and feet per second. Use a calculator to assist in your calculations. Round all answers to the nearest hundredth.

Average speed	Calculations	Kilometers per hour	Feet per second

NAME:______________________________ DATE:______________

LESSON 1.4

Common Core Assessment Practice

Directions: Complete the problems below.

1. A tank can hold 36 liters of water. If a valve pumps 3,000 mL of water into the tank every 30 minutes, how many hours will it take to fill the tank completely?
   a. 4
   b. 6
   c. 8
   d. 10

2. Mike's car broke down 5 miles from the auto shop. If he can push his car 1,056 feet per hour, how many hours will it take him to reach the auto shop?
   a. 25
   b. 30
   c. 35
   d. 40

3. A professional football wide receiver totaled 1,543 yards receiving during the 2014 season. How many feet is this receiving total?
   a. 2,975
   b. 3,765
   c. 4,235
   d. 4,629

4. Jules earned $360 working a 40-hour week at the local diner. How much money did she earn per minute?
   a. $0.12
   b. $0.14
   c. $0.15
   d. $0.18

5. Harold earns $11.50 an hour. If he works 35 hours a week for 50 weeks, how much money does Harold earn in one year?
   a. $12,150
   b. $20,125
   c. $25, 275
   d. $30,500

SECTION II

The Number System

LESSON 2.1

Fractions

Common Core State Standards

- 6.NS.A1

Mathematical Practices

- 1, 2, 3, 4, and 6

Estimated Time

- 60–90 minutes

Key Terms

- Fraction
- Reciprocal
- Numerator
- Denominator

Teacher's Note. It may make things go more smoothly if you have premeasured pieces of string or yarn that students can use to help them determine distances.

Materials

- Lesson 2.1 Activity: Fractions of a Class Change
- Lesson 2.1 Practice: Applications Using Fractions and Decimals
- Lesson 2.1 Common Core Assessment Practice
- Premeasured pieces of yarn (between 10–25 feet)
- Timer

Objectives

In this lesson, students will:

- interpret and compute quotients of fractions, decimals, and whole numbers.

Lesson 2.1 Activity: Fractions of a Class Change

Middle school students have a constant battle with the clock when changing classes. Teachers may believe students have more than enough time in the halls, whereas students will argue that they have a criminally short period between classes. Students will now have the opportunity to prove themselves right or wrong based on mathematical calculations using fractions.

Students will partner up and begin by measuring the distance they cover in a typical step. Students should write down the distance of their stride as a whole number (rounded), a decimal, and a fraction. Next, partners should make a list of their class changes and measure the distances they travel between classes.

After students have written down the distances they travel during their class changes, have students divide the distance between two classes by the distance covered in their stride to determine how many steps it will take to go from one class to the next. Students can then time each other to see how many steps they can take in 5 seconds and use that number to determine how long they need to get from one class to the next. When they have determined the time it takes them to travel that distance using their own steps, the students can compare the time to the allotted time for class changes.

NAME:______________________________ DATE:______________

LESSON 2.1 ACTIVITY

Fractions of a Class Change

Directions: How fair is your school's tardy policy? Do you think you and your classmates have enough time between classes? In this activity, you are about to prove it one way or another. Partner up with one of your classmates and begin working on a reasonable time to take when changing classes.

1. Measure the length of one of your (and your partner's) typical stride from the heel of one shoe to the toe of the other shoe. Write the length of this step in inches as a whole number (rounding if necessary), a decimal, and a fraction.

Your Stride (In Inches)	
a. Whole number:	________
b. Decimal:	________
c. Fraction:	________

Your Partner's Stride (In Inches)	
a. Whole number:	________
b. Decimal:	________
c. Fraction:	________

2. Make a list of class changes you have throughout the day. Choose two class changes (one of yours and one of your partner's). Use the premeasured pieces of string provided by your teacher to measure the distance from one class to the next. Figure out the total distance between each class change (in feet and in inches) and write it as a whole number (rounding if necessary), a decimal, and a fraction.

Your Class Change From ________ to ________	
In Feet	
a. Whole number:	________
b. Decimal:	________
c. Fraction:	________
In Inches	
a. Whole number:	________
b. Decimal:	________
c. Fraction:	________

Your Partner's Change From ________ to ________	
In Feet	
a. Whole number:	________
c. Decimal:	________
c. Fraction:	________
In Inches	
a. Whole number:	________
b. Decimal:	________
c. Fraction:	________

3. Figure out how many steps it will take you to move between classes (for both class changes) and write your answer as a whole number, a decimal, and a fraction.

Your Class Change From ____________ to ____________	
In Number of Steps	
a. Whole number:	____________
b. Decimal:	____________
c. Fraction:	____________

Your Partner's Change From ____________ to ____________	
In Number of Steps	
a. Whole number:	____________
b. Decimal:	____________
c. Fraction:	____________

4. Figure out how many steps you can take in 5 seconds with a typical pace: ____________ . Using that number, calculate how many seconds it will take you to make the class change. Write your answer as a whole number, a fraction, and a decimal.

Your Class Change From ____________ to ____________	
In Seconds	
a. Whole number:	____________
b. Decimal:	____________
c. Fraction:	____________

Your Partner's Change From ____________ to ____________	
In Seconds	
a. Whole number:	____________
b. Decimal:	____________
c. Fraction:	____________

5. Determine whether or not you have enough time between classes based on your calculations. Explain your answer.

Extend Your Thinking

1. Imagine that your principal is trying to put together schedules for the next school year. He wants student input on the different class changes that students might struggle to make in the allotted amount of time. With your partner, hypothesize and test different paths that students might take that would require a longer time than the amount allotted for class changes at your school. Show your calculations and write a brief petition to present your findings to your principal to make your case.

2. Calculate the distance you can travel by jogging for 5 seconds. Make a comparison between your typical pace and your jogging pace. Compare using a time period of 10 minutes. How much farther could you run than walk in 10 minutes? As a class, make a note of each of your different jogging times. If each person in the class were part of a relay team and each person jogged for 10 minutes, how far would the total distance traveled be for each student in your class put together?

NAME:________________________ DATE:____________

LESSON 2.1 PRACTICE

Applications Using Fractions and Decimals

Directions: Complete the problems below.

1. A farmer goes to a carpenter's workshop looking for fence posts. The carpenter shows him all 80 of the fence posts in his shop.
   a. The farmer tells the carpenter he will buy $\frac{4}{5}$ of the fence posts. How many fence posts did he buy?

   b. Each fence post is 4 feet high. The farmer measures and realizes he needs to cut 8.5 inches off the end of each post. How long is each post after the cut? Challenge: Write your measurement in inches and feet.

   c. The farmer's plan is to fence in a strip of his land for herding his cattle so that it forms a square. He decides to place the four corner posts of the fence and then place 15 posts in between each corner post so that there is a distance of $8\frac{1}{8}$ feet between each post around the entire fenced in area. Calculate the area and the perimeter of this fenced in area.

2. A deliveryman earns $0.75 for every mile that he drives.
   a. If the deliveryman has driven 45 and $\frac{3}{5}$ miles so far this morning, how much money has he earned?

   b. The deliveryman is trying to save his money to take his wife on a vacation. He calculates that he needs to earn $150 a day to save up for their vacation and pay for living expenses. How many more miles does he need to drive today to earn his $150?

c. The deliveryman and his wife worked out that he needs to set aside 18% of the $150 each day to fund their vacation. If he has been saving for 3 weeks (driving 5 days a week), how much has he saved?

d. The deliveryman had engine trouble one week and didn't get to save as much as he wanted that week. With the engine fixed, he has 5 days left until the vacation date. He still needs $210 dollars to meet his vacation budget. What percent of the $150 does he need to set aside each day this week (5 days) to meet his goal?

Extend Your Thinking

1. More and more health and fitness sites are suggesting that people walk 10,000 steps a day to maintain a healthy, active lifestyle. Using the normal pace that you calculated during Activity 2.1, figure out how long it would take you to walk 10,000 steps. How much total distance will you travel if you walk 10,000 steps?

2. Some physical education classes use pedometers in their lessons. Use a pedometer to see how many steps you take during a typical day and calculate the additional time and distance you would need to travel to reach the 10,000 step goal.

NAME:__________ DATE:__________

LESSON 2.1

Common Core Assessment Practice

Directions: Complete the problems below.

1. A recipe for brownies requires $4\frac{1}{2}$ cups of sugar and makes enough brownies for 12 people. If Yousef only wants to make brownies for 8 people, how many cups of sugar will he need for the recipe?
   - **a.** 9 cups
   - **b.** $2\frac{1}{8}$ cups
   - **c.** 3 cups
   - **d.** 8 cups

2. A relay race was $\frac{4}{5}$ of a mile long. If each person on the relay team had to run $\frac{1}{10}$ of a mile, how many people were on each relay team?
   - **a.** 4
   - **b.** 8
   - **c.** 10
   - **d.** 12

3. A farmer sections off 80% of his 20.45-acre farm for cotton. How many acres of cotton did he plant?
   - **a.** 16.36 acres
   - **b.** 4.09 acres
   - **c.** 16.5 acres
   - **d.** 18.24 acres

4. A pair of socks requires 0.75 feet of fabric to make. If a clothing manufacturer has 60.25 feet of fabric, how many socks can the manufacturer make?
   - **a.** 80 socks
   - **b.** 80.33 socks
   - **c.** 45 socks
   - **d.** 81 socks

5. A warehouse has 1,235 boxes of envelopes. Each delivery truck can hold 85 boxes of envelopes. How many trucks does the warehouse need to hire to ship all of its envelopes?
   - **a.** 14 trucks
   - **b.** 15 trucks
   - **c.** 16 trucks
   - **d.** 17 trucks

LESSON 2.2

Greatest Common Factor and Least Common Multiple

Common Core State Standards

- 6.NS.B.4

Mathematical Practices

- 1, 2, 3, 4, 8, and 9

Estimated Time

- 60–90 minutes

Key Terms

- Factor
- Multiple
- Prime factor (prime number)

Materials

- Lesson 2.2 Activity: Creating Monster Multiples
- Lesson 2.2 Number DNA
- Lesson 2.2 Zoo Identification Cards
- Lesson 2.2 Practice: Factors and Multiples
- Lesson 2.2 Common Core Assessment Practice
- Index cards
- Construction paper to create the monster multiples
- Lab coats (optional)
- Scientist wigs (optional)

Objectives

In this lesson, students will:

- find GCF values,
- find LCM values, and
- manipulate numbers by writing them as a product of a GCF.

Lesson 2.2 Activity: Creating Monster Multiples

Students will become mad scientists for this lesson. Assuming that the "DNA" of any number can be broken down into the product of its prime factors, students will create DNA mapping of two- and three-digit numbers by breaking them down into prime factors. Students will find a partner whose number shares a common factor and then "splice" the DNA of two or more numbers to create mutant multiples (the LCM of the two numbers). For example, one student may receive the number 234 and another may receive 270. The GCF that they share is 18. By factoring out the 18 from each number, students will notice that the "unique DNA" between the two numbers is 13 and 15. Students will splice that DNA to make a monster with a genetic makeup of 18 (13 x 15), or the LCM of the two numbers. Students can create a monster avatar for the monster number that they have created.

As students finish creating their monster numbers, the class will create a monster numbers zoo by grouping each of the numbers into common species, where the species is the GCF that a group of numbers share. For example, the numbers 4,320 and 3,744 have a GCF of 288, but when they are grouped with 4,104 and 6,426, all four numbers share a GCF of 18; thus, they would be grouped in the species 18. Students should use the DNA map for each number to help them figure out in which species their monster number belongs. Using the numbers above, 4,320 has a DNA map of $2^5 \times 3^3 \times 5$; 3,744 has a DNA map of $2^5 \times 3^2 \times 13$; 4,104 has a DNA map of $2^3 \times 3^3 \times 19$; and 6,426 has a DNA map of $2^1 \times 3^3 \times 7 \times 17$. Looking over all four numbers, you can see that they only share one 2 and two 3s. Multiply them together and you get 18. As students are creating the zoo, each monster number should come with an identification card that indicates from which two (or multiple numbers) the monster was created. For example, the LCM of 270 and 375 is 6,750 (the monster number created from splicing the DNA of 270 and 375). The zoo identification card would read 15 (18 x 25) to indicate the common DNA that the two numbers share and the different DNA (18 and 25) that are being spliced together to form the monster.

Teacher's Note. It may be easier to already have your exhibits of numbers planned out before assigning the numbers to students so you know which numbers are supposed to group with other numbers.

NAME:______________________________ DATE:______________

LESSON 2.2 ACTIVITY

Creating Monster Multiples

Directions: Mad scientists wanted! You are needed to create a monster number for a new zoo opening in your area. Because you have a great understanding of a number's DNA, the zoo needs you to create a monster number by combining two or more numbers' DNA.

1. Your teacher will assign you one number, most likely a two- or three-digit number that you might find in the wild. Create a DNA map of the number by completing a prime factorization for your number. Complete Lesson 2.2 Number DNA handout to record your scientific findings.

2. Compare the DNA map of your number to that of the other mad scientists around you (your classmates). Find numbers that share a common factor or GCF. You and your partner will then "splice" the unique DNA of one number (all of the prime factors left after the GCF is taken out) with the unique DNA of the other number to create a monster multiple.

3. When you have created your monster multiple, design a monster to represent this monster multiple using your construction paper.

4. Create a zoo identification card using Lesson 2.2 Zoo Identification Cards handout. Identify the GCF of the two numbers you spliced and the unique DNA that you combined to form your monster. For example, 36 and 48 share a GCF of 12. The unique DNA left would be 3 and 4, respectively. The zoo identification card would be 12 (3 x 4) to indicate that 12 is the DNA shared and that 3 and 4 are the unique DNA spliced together to create the monster multiple of 144. Then write a brief description of your Monster Multiple: natural habitats, types of behaviors your multiple might exhibit, and so forth (be creative!).

5. Group your numbers into common exhibits by displaying the numbers who share the monster multiples that share the same GCFs.

Extend Your Thinking

1. You can "visit" the zoo by walking around and looking at the identification cards. You should try to notice patterns in each of the different species (numbers who share the same GCF). Generalize a rule for numbers who share the same GCFs. For example, you might notice that monster numbers formed between numbers who share the GCF of 15 will end in either a 5 or a 0. Try to make connections between the patterns that you notice and the GCF of the monster numbers.

2. Some monster numbers may be caught in the wild and brought to the zoo for safekeeping. It is your job to correctly classify these wild monster numbers. You will receive four- and five-digit numbers and break down each number's DNA to find in which GCF section of the zoo the number should go and what two numbers were spliced together to form the monster number (with some numbers the answers might vary and you can discuss why that is).

NAME:______________________________ DATE:______________

LESSON 2.2
Number DNA

First Number: ______________________________

List of prime numbers that make up the "DNA" of your number (list repeated prime numbers). Construct a factor tree in the space below (other methods can also be substituted).

Number DNA (prime factorization of your number): ______________________________

NAME: ______________________ DATE: ______________

LESSON 2.2

Zoo Identification Cards

Monster Multiple 1

(Picture Here)	**Name:** **Species (common GCF):** **DNA Makeup (GCF and product of unique DNA):**
Description:	

Monster Multiple 2

(Picture Here)	**Name:** **Species (common GCF):** **DNA Makeup (GCF and product of unique DNA):**
Description:	

NAME:______________________________ DATE:______________

LESSON 2.2 PRACTICE

Factors and Multiples

Directions: Complete the problems below.

1. A baker has 45 muffins and 60 rolls. He wants to make bags of muffins and rolls so that each bag has the same number of muffins and the same number of rolls with none being left over.
   a. What are the possible numbers of bags he can make?

   b. What is the greatest number of bags he can make?

   c. How many muffins and rolls will be in each bag if he makes the greatest number of bags possible?

2. Judith and Augustina are running laps around the lake. They both start at the same time and go in the same direction. Judith completes a lap every 4 minutes and Augustina completes a lap every 6 minutes.
   a. If they just started, how many minutes will it be before they are both at the starting line at the same time again?

   b. If they both run for 60 minutes, how many times will they meet up at the starting line during their run?

   c. During that 60-minute time period, how many laps will Judith have run and how many laps will Augustina have run?

Extend Your Thinking

1. It is your job to create a taxonomy of monster numbers. Be as creative as you like in your classifications. For example, all numbers have a factor of 1, so that might be the kingdom in which all monster numbers are classified. You can then group numbers into phylum, class, order, family, genus, and species as you see fit. You can then compare your classification systems to each other and see where you agreed and differed. Discuss the reasons why you chose your classification system with other groups in your class.

NAME:______________________________ DATE:______________

LESSON 2.2
Common Core Assessment Practice

Directions: Complete the problems below.

1. A florist is making flower bouquets out of pink and purple roses. The florist has 80 pink roses and 120 purple roses. What is the greatest number of bouquets the florist can make so that each bouquet has the same number of pink and purple roses and no roses are left over?
   a. 12
   b. 20
   c. 40
   d. 80

2. What is the smallest possible number that is divisible by both 16 and 24?
   a. 16
   b. 24
   c. 36
   d. 48

3. Justin goes hiking every 8 days. Joel goes hiking every 10 days. If they just hiked together on the same day, how many days will it be before they both hike on the same day again?
   a. 2 days
   b. 40 days
   c. 80 days
   d. 120 days

4. The Necklace Depot sells necklace charms in packs of 10. The Lovely Necklace sells necklace charms in packs of 15. At the end of the day, both stores sold the same number of necklace charms. Which of the following could be the number of charms they sold that day?
   a. 20
   b. 45
   c. 160
   d. 330

5. Horace has 50 pens and 75 pencils. He wants to make packs of writing utensils so that each pack has the same number of pens and the same number of pencils while making sure to use all of the pens and pencils available. If Horace made the greatest possible number of packs of pencils and pens, how many pencils were in each pack?
   a. 3
   b. 5
   c. 10
   d. 25

LESSON 2.3

Positive and Negative Numbers

Common Core State Standards

- 6.NS.C.5
- 6.NS.C.6a

Mathematical Practices

- 1, 2, 3, 4, 6, and 7

Estimated Time

- 60–90 minutes

Key Terms

- Integer
- Positive number
- Negative number
- Narrative poem

Materials

- Lesson 2.3 Activity: Positive and Negative Narrative
- Lesson 2.3 Positive and Negative Narrative Poem
- Lesson 2.3 Narrative Poem Worksheet
- Lesson 2.3 Practice: Using Positive and Negative Numbers
- Lesson 2.3 Common Core Assessment Practice
- Markers

Objectives

In this lesson, students will:

- understand that positive and negative numbers are used together to describe quantities having opposite directions,
- use positive and negative numbers to represent real-world quantities,
- identify the meaning of zero in each real-world situation, and
- recognize opposite signs of numbers indicate opposites on a number line.

Lesson 2.3 Activity: Positive and Negative Narrative

Students will begin the lesson by reading through Lesson 2.3 Positive and Negative Narrative Poem. While reading the poem and completing Lesson 2.3 Narrative Poem Worksheet, students will identify language in the narration that indicates positive or negative numbers. Students will keep track of the positive and negative numbers and how they move based on the language. Finally, students will identify the resolution of the poem when both the positive and negative numbers become opposites.

After students have gone through the provided narrative, students will write their own narrative poem (a short story can also be substituted). Students will have to think of situations where positive and negative numbers might be used in real or fantasy situations. In their narrative poems, students will tie the positive and negative number language to the characters and conflict in the story to help the plot of the narrative move forward. As with the provided example poem, the students will resolve their poem when a positive number and negative number become opposites.

NAME:_______________________________________ DATE:_______________

LESSON 2.3 ACTIVITY

Positive and Negative Narrative

Directions: Think you can find the positives and negatives in a poem? Sure, it's easy to find what you like and dislike, but can you track a number throughout a poem and find the language that changes in ways positive or negative? Follow the directions below.

1. Read Lesson 2.3 Positive and Negative Narrative Poem. Highlight (in different colors) language in the poem that signifies positive and negative values or changes to a number.

2. Complete Lesson 2.3 Narrative Poem Worksheet.

Extend Your Thinking

1. Create a number line to track the movements of two of the numbers (one positive, one negative) throughout the length of the narrative poem or short story that you write. Use a green marker to track positive changes and a red marker to track negative changes. Circle with a blue marker the point(s) when there are two points on the number line that are opposites.

2. Look through your number line and turn the positive and negative movements of the numbers into addition and subtraction operations. Write the operations with the starting number and the movement (positive or negative) and the resulting number. For example, if a temperature (in Celsius) starts at negative 14 (-14) and drops 4 degrees, the operation would be $-14 - 4 = -18$ degrees. After writing the operations out, try to generalize rules about adding and subtracting with negative numbers.

NAME:____ DATE:____________________

LESSON 2.3

Positive and Negative Narrative Poem

Directions: As you read the poem, highlight words that indicate positive or negative temperatures.

The sun splintered down on the tundra below
A warmth filled the air and the temperature rose
It climbed and it climbed some 15 degrees
There was hardly a sign of the danger, the freeze.
Bartholomew worked in his Antarctic lab
Testing the ice, slab after slab
Bristled and burned, his fingers afire
He was beginning to slow; he was beginning to tire
Careless, an ice block fell to the floor
It shattered and fractured into pieces galore
Out of the core of ice rose a harsh scream
And the pieces that scattered all melted to steam
The lights in the lab went instantly black
The temperature plunged 40 degrees with a crack
Bartholomew, frightened, threw on his jacket
And ran out the door to escape all the racket
By the time he looked up the sun was scarce to be found
His feet slipped and he slid over the ice-covered ground
Shaking all over, he looked with a shock
The temperature outside had dropped like a rock
Well below zero, it continued to fall
It fell 30 degrees before beginning to stall
Worn down and wearied he ran from the air
He started a fire with one of his flares
With the flame from the flare he warmed up his toes
He heated his hands and thawed out his nose
The air warmed around him from the heat and the glow
Twenty-five degrees warmer though still very low
Bartholomew saw and realized with fear
The flare's light was waning and the warmth's end was near.
Before the light faded he looked at his gauge
"Seventy-five below zero," he read with great rage
The dark closed around him and he let out a scream
He woke with a start and realized it was all just a dream
Bartholomew read the thermometer clear
It read 75 degrees, and he shouted a cheer.

NAME:______________________________ DATE:______________

LESSON 2.3

Narrative Poem Worksheet

Directions: Use the narrative poem to answer Questions 1–3.

1. **a.** What were some of the highlighted words in the poem that indicated positive or negative temperatures?

   b. How did you know they indicated positive or negative temperatures?

2. Write the temperatures in the poem as integer values. On the poem, track the numbers as they increase or decrease based on positive or negative wording.

3. Make notes as the numbers change and mark the resolution of the story when the numbers become opposites. Which values in the poem were opposites? Explain how you know they are opposites.

4. Now it is your turn. Think of real-life situations (or fantastical situations) where positive and negative numbers can be used. What is the topic on which your want to write your narrative poem or short story?

5. Brainstorm a storyline that can incorporate those real-life situations into the plot. List some keywords related to your topic that indicate positive or negative values. For example, if you are using temperature, you can use words like falling, rising, cooling, or warming in your story.

Positive: **Negative:**

6. Write your own narrative poem or short story where the negative and positive integers change as part of the story's conflict or based on the characters in the story and their actions. Use different terminology in your story to indicate positive and negative changes to numbers.

7. As a resolution, you should have at least one pair of integers become opposites as a result of the plot of the story. For example, at the end of a story, a bird might rise to a height of 35 m and a dolphin might dive to 35 m below sea level (or -35 m), which is where the story would end.

NAME:______________________________ DATE:______________

LESSON 2.3 PRACTICE

Using Positive and Negative Numbers

Directions: Complete the problems below.

1. On a climb of K2, the mountaineers began their day 22,450 feet above sea level. They made an ascent of 1,500 feet before descending to 21,250 feet to acclimatize.
   a. Assign an integer value to their ascent and descent.

   b. Calculate the net gain/loss of altitude on this day of climbing.

   c. The climbers spend the next 5 days ascending from 21,250 feet to 26,500 feet. What was the average ascent per day during this stretch?

   d. The climbers then summit to 28,251 feet. They spend the next 30 minutes at the summit before descending back down the mountain to 26,500 feet. What was the net gain of altitude during this climb?

   e. The next day the climbers descend to 20,500 feet. What integer can represent this descent?

2. Camille opened a bank account and deposited $1,500.
   a. Write this value as an integer.

   b. Camille spends $750 on a plane ticket to Paris, France. How much money does she have in her account now? Represent this purchase as an integer value.

   c. She decides to spend $250 a night on a hotel for 5 nights. Write an integer value to represent the value of her bank account now.

Extend Your Thinking

1. Research the average high and low temperature for a month in your town. This should be one monthly high and one monthly low (calculate the average if needed). Track the current temperature over a week and compare it to the average monthly temperature using positive and negative numbers. As you assign a positive or negative number to each temperature, create a bar graph to represent the current temperature as it compares to the average. Consider the x-axis (horizontal axis) of your bar graph to be the average monthly temperature. Negative values should fall below that line, while positive values should be above that line.

NAME:______________________________ DATE:______________

LESSON 2.3

Common Core Assessment Practice

Directions: Complete the problems below.

1. If Galen has less than -$30 on his credit card, which of the following values can represent the amount of money he has?
   a. -$25
   b. $25
   c. $35
   d. -$42

2. Jonathan starts from his house and travels east 35.8 miles. He then travels west 42.2 miles. How far is he from his house?
   a. 6.4 miles
   b. 78 miles
   c. -7.6 miles
   d. 7.6 miles

3. Charlotte is diving from a 30-foot-high diving board. What integer value can represent the distance from the surface of the water she needs to reach to be opposite of the height of the diving board?
   a. -30 feet
   b. 30 feet
   c. 15 feet
   d. 60 feet

4. Which of the following situations would not represent -5?
   a. A temperature fall of 5 degrees
   b. A deposit of $5
   c. A loss by 5 points
   d. Snorkeling 5 feet underwater

5. Starting from an elevation of 45 degrees below sea level a diver rose 30 feet. Represent the diver's new elevation as an integer.
   a. 15
   b. -15
   c. 75
   d. -75

LESSON 2.4

The Coordinate Plane

Common Core State Standards

- 6.NS.C.6b
- 6.NS.C.6c
- 6.NS.C.8

Mathematical Practices

- 1, 2, 3, 4, 5, and 6

Estimated Time

- 60–90 minutes

Key Terms

- Y-axis and x-axis
- Coordinate plane
- Coordinates
- Origin
- Ordered pair

Materials

- Lesson 2.4 Activity: Mapping a Novel
- Lesson 2.4 Coordinate Grid Setting Map
- Lesson 2.4 Setting Map
- Lesson 2.4 Practice: Coordinate Grids
- Lesson 2.4 Common Core Assessment Practice
- *Hatchet* by Gary Paulsen (optional)
- Ruler
- Grid paper
- Map of continental United States (for extension)

Objectives

In this lesson, students will:

- understand how ordered pairs indicate locations in quadrants of a coordinate plane,
- find and position integers on a coordinate plane, and
- solve real-world problems by graphing points on a coordinate plane and using absolute value to find the distance between two points.

Lesson 2.4 Activity: Mapping a Novel

Teacher's Note. A suggested book for this lesson is *Hatchet* by Gary Paulsen, which is aligned with the 6–8 Common Core State Standards for ELA. This lesson can be adapted to other stories or even used with creating a map of the school's campus or other area familiar to your classes.

In this activity, students will create a map on a coordinate plane based on key locations in the book. Students should create their coordinate map on the Lesson 2.4 Coordinate Grid Setting Map handout. Students will decide which location is the most central for the story and use this location as the origin on the coordinate plane. Every other location mapped out will be based on its position relative to the central location. If the location that is central to the plot changes during the story, students can base their coordinate plane on just one part of the story instead of the entire novel. Students should use descriptions in the novel to estimate how far each location is from the central location. Students should also understand that locations can be in any area surrounding the central location and should use cardinal directions (north, south, east, and west) to visualize where each location might be relative to that position. As students determine the key locations in the story and their position relative to the central location (origin), students will mark a point on the coordinate plane for each place in the story and note the ordered pair that accompanies the place.

Obviously stories are not spaced out in a grid-like manner, and students should be encouraged to estimate distances and locations based on evidence in the book. Encourage students to imagine a panorama or 360-degree view of the surrounding area and to think about what they visualize based on imagery in the story. Also, the locations chosen don't need to be actual landmarks. For example, *Hatchet* is set in a Canadian forest. Because there may not be distinctive features to separate parts of the forest, students should think about the locations of events that happen within the forest and the distance they were from the central location. They can then label the position on the coordinate plane as an event or conflict instead of a landmark.

After students have created their coordinate plane map of the book on the Lesson 2.4 Coordinate Grid Setting Map, students should complete the Lesson 2.4 Setting Map handout. This handout will ask them to find the distances (based on the point's ordered pair) between locations. Students might notice that some points are at angles from other locations. Students should understand that they cannot (yet) determine the length of a diagonal line on a grid and to figure out a means to determine the length traveled by using two straight lines to connect the points.

Teacher's Note. For your more creative/artistic students, you could have them create their own setting map and design it to look like the setting of the novel they are using. You can also encourage students to use a 3-D model of the important events of the story as the points on the coordinate grid. For example, students may choose to build a fire to represent Brian's shelter in *Hatchet*. They can place the model of the fire on the point of the grid that represents his shelter.

NAME:______________________________ DATE:______________

LESSON 2.4 ACTIVITY

Mapping a Novel

Directions: How well do you know your favorite book? Can you visualize all of the important locations of this book? Create a map of the central setting to your favorite book by plotting the important points on a coordinate grid based on text evidence from the book. This coordinate map should help a future reader better visualize the events of the book as the character(s) move from one place to the next.

1. Determine the central location or most important location in your story (or in the part of your story on which you are focusing). This is the origin on your coordinate plane. For example, if you are reading a Harry Potter novel, the central location might be Hogwarts School of Witchcraft and Wizardry (or a specific area inside the castle).
2. Determine 7–10 specific locations to which the character(s) travel that are located around your central location. Use context clues from the book to determine a direction and distance from your central location at which this point is located. Try to simplify directions to varying degrees of north, south, east, and west.
3. Using your direction and distance relative to the origin, plot each specific location on your Lesson 2.4 Coordinate Grid Setting Map worksheet as a point with a specific ordered pair.
4. To identify each specific location, list the ordered pair, a name for the location, and a brief text description of the location for each point on your map (including the origin). For example, you might identify the origin as (0, 0) as Hogwarts and a brief text description about the castle.
5. Complete your Lesson 2.4 Setting Map worksheet by identifying specific locations and their ordered pairs and using absolute value to calculate the distances between points on your map.
6. Keep in mind that locations on your map could be related to an event or conflict in the story and not necessarily linked to a specific landmark.

Extend Your Thinking

1. Think about which unit of measure would be appropriate for determining the distance between the points on your map and create a scale to represent that unit of measure. This will, of course, be an estimate, but you should try to use your scale to make an educated guess for how far the character traveled during the story in the book. If you only focused on a specific set of chapters in the book, you can limit your distance-traveled calculations to that part of the book.
2. Look through the descriptions in the story as a character is moving from one point to another. Make a note of parts of imagery that are mentioned in this journey. Add these images to your Lesson 2.4 Setting Map worksheet using fraction or decimal ordered pairs and calculate the corresponding distances between major points on your map and these newly added descriptions.

NAME:__________ DATE:__________

LESSON 2.4

Coordinate Grid Setting Map

Directions: Using the coordinate grid below, represent a point on the grid for every important location/event in the novel you are reading.

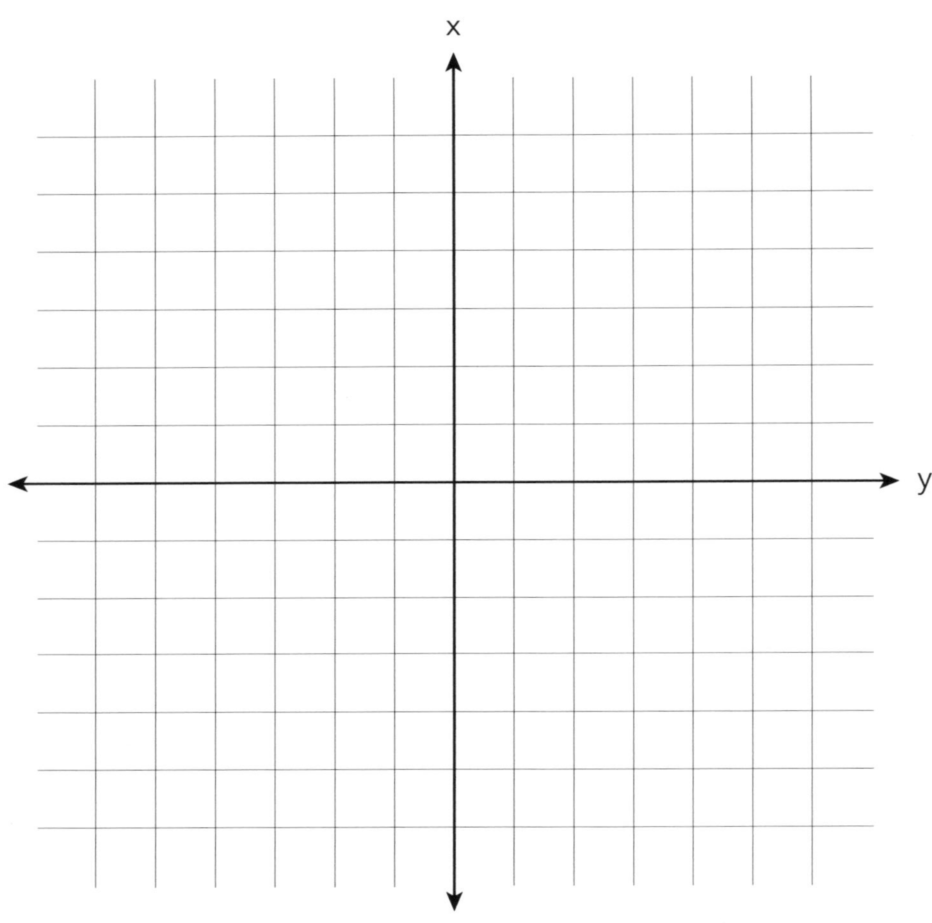

NAME:______________________________ DATE:______________

LESSON 2.4

Setting Map

Directions: Use the coordinate grid you made on the Lesson 2.4 Coordinate Grid Setting Map handout to complete the following worksheet. List the locations/events you placed on your grid and their corresponding ordered pair. Let Point A be your central location (origin).

Point A: ____________ Ordered Pair: (______ , ______)

Point B: ____________ Ordered Pair: (______ , ______)

Point C: ____________ Ordered Pair: (______ , ______)

Point D: ____________ Ordered Pair: (______ , ______)

Point E: ____________ Ordered Pair: (______ , ______)

Point F: ____________ Ordered Pair: (______ , ______)

Point G: ____________ Ordered Pair: (______ , ______)

1. What is the distance from Point A to Point B? ____________

2. What is the distance from Point E to Point G? ____________

3. What is the distance from Point C to Point F? ____________

4. What is the distance from Point B to Point C? ____________

5. At one point in your story's plot, your character probably travels through a series of places or events. Describe the journey that your character takes at one point in the story and then use your corresponding points to calculate the distance your character would have traveled during this journey.

NAME:______________________________ DATE:______________

LESSON 2.4 PRACTICE

Coordinate Grids

Directions: Complete the problems below.

1. Caleb is starting a paper route. He sits down at his desk and begins mapping out the route. He starts at his house and travels west 3 blocks. He delivers his first paper to Mrs. Peterson before turning north.
   a. If his house represents the origin on a graph, what ordered pair will represent Mrs. Peterson's house?

   b. Explain how you determined the ordered pair for Part A.

   c. Caleb turns north from Mrs. Peterson's house and travels 5 blocks. During the 5 blocks, he delivers 10 papers. Create ordered pairs that might represent these 10 houses. Justify your answers for these ordered pairs.

   d. Caleb then turns east and travels 5 blocks. If he is finished with his route, write the directions for him to get back to his house from here without turning around and going back the way he came.

The Number System

e. If each block is 0.25 of a mile, how far does Caleb ride during his route?

2. Porter is marking important locations on a graph. He marks his house at (0, 0). He marks his school at (4, 5). He marks the library at (-3, 6), his favorite restaurant at (-3, -4), and his basketball gym at (0, 6).
   a. If each point on the graph represents one mile, how far is it from his house to the gym?

   b. How far is it from the gym to the library?

   c. How far is it from the library to the restaurant?

   d. If Porter starts at school, then goes to the library, then out to eat, then to the gym, and finally back home, how far does he travel if he can only move up, down, left, or right on the graph?

Extend Your Thinking

1. You have received a map of the continental United States from your teacher. Place a grid over it and plot the major cities on the grid using ordered pairs. Using the scale and the ordered pairs, estimate distances between cities based on absolute value calculations. Compare the estimated distances to the actual distances between the cities. Explain what you think could cause the discrepancies between the estimated distance and the actual distance between cities.

NAME:______________________________ DATE:______________

LESSON 2.4

Common Core Assessment Practice

Directions: Complete the problems below.

1. On a map, the bank is located at the coordinates (3, 8) and the mall is located at (3, -4). How far is the bank from the mall?
   a. 8 units
   b. 4 units
   c. 3 units
   d. 12 units

2. A hunter sets up camp in the woods. He travels 3 miles east, 5 miles north, and then 2 miles west to his deer stand. If his camp is the origin, on which coordinates is his deer stand?
   a. (1, 5)
   b. (3, 5)
   c. (-2, 3)
   d. (5, 3)

3. In which quadrant is the ordered pair (-5, 12) located?
   a. Quadrant I
   b. Quadrant II
   c. Quadrant III
   d. Quadrant IV

4. A house is located at the point (-2, 8.5) on a coordinate map. Another house is located on the point (-2, -6.25). How far away are the two houses from each other?
   a. -2 units
   b. 2.25 units
   c. 8.5 units
   d. 14.75 units

5. A train's route is mapped out on a coordinate grid. The main train station is located at the origin. Each stop is located every 0.25 units on the coordinate grid. If the train is currently at the point (0, 5) how many stops away from the main train station is it?
   a. 20 stops
   b. 15 stops
   c. 10 stops
   d. 5 stops

LESSON 2.5

Absolute Value

Common Core State Standards

- 6.NS.C.7a–d

Mathematical Practices

- 1, 2, 3, 4, 6, and 9

Estimated Time

- 90–120 minutes

Key Terms

- Absolute value
- Opposites
- Inequality

Materials

- Lesson 2.5 Activity: Absolute Value of a Skyline
- Lesson 2.5 Absolute Value Skyline Worksheet
- Lesson 2.5 Practice: Applications of Absolute Value
- Lesson 2.5 Common Core Assessment Practice
- Shoebox
- String or yarn
- LEGOs or other building blocks (a variety of building materials, such as Popsicle sticks or modeling clay, may be substituted)

Objectives

In this lesson, students will:

- understand the absolute value of rational numbers,
- understand that the absolute value of a rational number is its distance from 0,
- distinguish statements of absolute value from statements about order, and
- write, interpret, and explain statements of order for rational numbers in real-world contexts.

Lesson 2.5 Activity: Absolute Value of a Skyline

Students will begin the lesson by researching the heights of the top 10 (can be more or less) tallest buildings in major cities around the world with a partner. They will calculate the average height of those 10 buildings. Students will then create a number line where zero (0) is the average height of the buildings and assign positive or negative integers to the 10 buildings based on their height compared to the average. For example, if the average height of the 10 buildings is 500 m, and one building is 550 m, that building has an integer value of +50. Conversely, if a building has a height of 450 m, that building has an integer value of -50.

Students will construct a diorama of their skyline showing the average (as zero on a number line) and the heights of each building in relation to the average height. The students should label each building with its actual height and its integer value written as an absolute value to show its distance from zero.

After students finish their diorama, they will answer questions about their city's skyline and the relationship that the buildings have to the ground, the average height, and each other.

NAME:____ DATE:_______________

LESSON 2.5 ACTIVITY

Absolute Value of a Skyline

Directions: Cities become famous for their skylines. Have you ever seen pictures of New York, Chicago, or even Hong Kong? Clusters of massive skyscrapers that dominate the horizon are a testament to the ingenuity and imagination of the human spirit. But exactly how tall are these buildings, and how does their height relate to the tallest buildings in your town or city? With your partner, you will be choosing a major city from around the world and create a diorama so you can visually represent the relationship between the heights of the buildings.

1. Choose one of the largest cities from around the world, including the United States.

2. Make a list of the top 10 tallest buildings in that city as well as the height of the buildings.

3. Calculate the average height of the 10 buildings you researched. This value is your zero (0) value on your number line.

4. Measure the height of this average on your shoebox to begin your diorama. Use a scale of 1 inch = 100 m or 1 inch = 500 feet (feel free to adjust the scale as needed, just make sure you are consistent). Tie your piece of string/yarn across the face of the box to mark the zero on your number line. Remember, the zero line should be the average height of the 10 buildings.

5. Assign an integer value based on each building's height compared to the average height of all of the buildings. A building that is taller than the average will have a positive number, and a building that is shorter will have a negative number.

6. Build your diorama by constructing models for each of your buildings in your diorama. On each building label the height and show the absolute value of the building based on its distance from the average height. Make sure your buildings are constructed to scale.

7. Complete the Lesson 2.5 Absolute Value Skyline Worksheet.

Extend Your Thinking

1. Compare your diorama and buildings from your skyline to other groups in the class. With the other groups in the class, create a number line that orders the heights of the top three buildings from each group in the class. Make sure you also order the buildings by the assigned integers and compare buildings by how they relate to the average height of the skylines. Notice how the rankings of buildings differ.

2. As a class, measure each person's height in feet (write the numbers as mixed fractions). Find the average height of the class and determine an absolute value for each person in the class. These absolute values should be written as a fraction and as a decimal (rounded to the nearest hundredth if necessary). You can assign a negative absolute value to those students who are shorter than the class average and a positive absolute value for those who are taller. Discuss any observations you and your classmates might have about how to order the absolute value of negative and positive fractions.

NAME:________________________________ DATE:________________

LESSON 2.5 ACTIVITY

Absolute Value Skyline Worksheet

Directions: Use your research on your city's skyline to complete the worksheet.

1. List the heights of the tallest 10 buildings in your city.

   1st ________ 2nd ________ 3rd ________ 4th ________ 5th ________

   6th ________ 7th ________ 8th ________ 9th ________ 10th ________

2. What is the average height of those 10 buildings?

3. Write an absolute value to represent the distance each of the 10 buildings is from the average height.

   1st ________ 2nd ________ 3rd ________ 4th ________ 5th ________

   6th ________ 7th ________ 8th ________ 9th ________ 10th ________

4. What is the height of the tallest building in your hometown? ________________

5. Write an absolute value to represent how your hometown's tallest building compares to the average height of the buildings in the city you researched.

6. Choose the shortest and tallest buildings in your hometown's skyline. Explain how the two absolute values used to represent their respective heights relate to the difference in the two buildings' actual heights.

7. Explain how absolute values might be used to find the difference between a positive and negative number.

NAME:________________________________ DATE:____________

LESSON 2.5 PRACTICE

Applications of Absolute Value

Directions: Complete the problems below.

1. The average height in a class of sixth graders is 50.2 inches.
   a. If a student is 58.6 inches tall, what absolute value could be written to represent the distance that his height is from the average in the class?

   b. Another student is 42.7 inches tall. What absolute value could be written to represent the distance she is from the average height in the class?

   c. If a student is 56.8 inches tall, what would be considered her opposite height, using the average heights for the class?

2. Three groups of hikers are on Annapurna trying for a summit bid. Group 1 is at a camp (Camp 3) at 23,354 feet. Group 2 is waiting somewhat higher, planning to try for the summit tomorrow. They are at Camp 4, which is right at 25,500 feet. The third group has left Camp 4 for the summit and is climbing at 26,235 feet.
   a. If Camp 4 is the average starting point for a summit try, write an absolute value to represent the distance each of the three groups is from Camp 4.

b. Group 3 begins its descent from the summit. When the group members get to 25,854 feet, they are opposite of Group 1 from Camp 4. What is the altitude of Group 1?

c. Group 2 began its summit try that morning. Group 2 reaches the summit of 26,545 feet at 10 a.m. Write an absolute value that represents the distance ascended from Camp 4.

d. At 2 p.m. that same day, the altitude of Group 1 can be written as |-50|, the altitude of Group 2 can be written as |945|, and the altitude of Group 3 can be written as |-1,254|. What are the actual altitudes of all three groups?

Extend Your Thinking

1. Begin by measuring the height from the floor to the ceiling in a room. Your height will serve as the zero value on the number line. Make a list of items that are located below you in the room and above you in the room. Measure the heights of these objects and place them accordingly on the number line where objects that are above you are positive and items below you are negative. When you are measuring items, the assigned number should be determined by the distance that item is from your height (which is serving as zero in this situation) not the distance the item is from the floor. You will then calculate the absolute value of the items after ordering them on the number line, making note of which items are opposites.

NAME:______________________________ DATE:______________

LESSON 2.5

Common Core Assessment Practice

Directions: Complete the problems below.

1. A submarine is currently cruising at 300 feet below sea level. Which absolute value correctly identifies the distance the submarine is from sea level?
   a. | 300|
   b. | -300|
   c. 300
   d. -300

2. Cody plots two points: (3, 16) and (3, -12). Which of the following two points are the same distance as the two Cody plotted?
   a. (3, 16) and (3, 12)
   b. (15, 6) and (-13, 8)
   c. (12, 10) and (-12, -18)
   d. (0, 20) and (0, -8)

3. The perimeter of a rectangle is 28. The base of the rectangle is formed by Point A (-6, 8) and Point B (4, 8). Which of the following points could form the height of the rectangle?
   a. (8, 8)
   b. (-10, 8)
   c. (4, 12)
   d. (-6, -4)

4. A student is given a piece of graph paper with a point marked at the coordinates (-2, -6). The student is told to draw a line up 9 units and place a point there. What are the coordinate points for the new point?
   a. (-8, 6)
   b. (7, -6)
   c. (-2, 3)
   d. (-2, 15)

5. A student is given a point at the origin and told to form a square by drawing a point four units left of the origin and drawing a point four units down from the origin. What are the coordinate for the fourth point that completes the square?
   a. (4, 4)
   b. (4, -4)
   c. (-4, 4)
   d. (-4, -4)

SECTION III

Expressions and Equations

LESSON 3.1

Working With Exponents and Exponential Expressions

Common Core State Standards

- 6.EE.A.1

Mathematical Practices

- 1, 2, 7, and 8

Estimated Time

- 60–90 minutes

Key Terms

- Expression
- Exponent
- Equivalent

Materials

- Lesson 3.1 Activity: Power of a Collage
- Lesson 3.1 Expression Brainstorm Sheet
- Lesson 3.1 Practice: Exponential Expressions
- Lesson 3.1 Common Core Assessment Practice
- Old magazines/newspapers or construction paper
- Blank paper (any size is fine; the larger the size, the longer the activity)

Objectives

In this lesson, students will:

- write mathematical expressions using exponents.

Lesson 3.1 Activity: Power of a Collage

This lesson provides a way for students to use exponents in expressions. Students will begin by dividing their blank sheet of paper (it can be as large or as small as you want) into four equal boxes. Students will write a single-digit number, a two-digit number, a three-digit number, and a four-digit number on the paper. Each number goes into the center of one of the four boxes until all four boxes have a number. Then, students will brainstorm ways to write exponential expressions to represent each of the four numbers. Students should record these on the Brainstorm Sheet. Every term in the expressions needs to be written as a whole number exponent, and students should use all four basic operations in their expressions. For example, if one of the numbers in a box is 3, some possible expressions the students could use would be $2^2 - 6^0$ or $9^2 \div 3^3$.

Once students have brainstormed all of their expressions, they should begin forming the expressions and pasting them in the boxes around their numbers. Students can either cut the expressions out of construction paper or cut out the necessary numbers from the magazines or newspapers. Because operation signs might be scarce, encourage students to use key operational words in their expressions or create their own operation signs to add to their expressions. These expressions should be pasted around the numbers in the boxes as a collage. All of the expressions should simplify to the number in the center of each box.

NAME:____ DATE:______________

LESSON 3.1 ACTIVITY

Power of a Collage

Directions: How many different ways are there to write a number? In this activity, you will represent numbers by writing operations with different bases and exponents.

1. Fold your paper so that it is divided into four equal boxes.

2. Choose a single-digit number and write it in the middle of one of the rectangles. Do the same for a two-digit, three-digit, and four-digit number.

3. Think of different ways you can use exponents in operations to come up with the four numbers that you have written. Brainstorm as many of these ways as possible. For example, the number 1 can be written as $2^2 - 3^1$ or $4^2 \div 2^4$.

4. After you have brainstormed and have written a number of expressions on the brainstorm sheet, begin cutting out numbers from your magazines or newspapers and construct the expressions using these cutouts. The different operation signs may be difficult to find in magazines and newspapers, so you can find word equivalents. For example, you could find "minus" or "less" to indicate subtraction.

5. Paste these expressions into each of the different squares to create a collage of equivalent exponential expressions.

Extend Your Thinking

1. Create flash cards for your partner. On each flash card, write three exponential expressions where you are operating with exponents. All three of these expressions, though different, should equal the same integer. Write that integer on the back of your card as the answer. Show the card(s) to your partner and ask him or her to figure out the answer on the back by solving the three expressions on the front.

2. Have a classmate or your teacher give you two different fractions. Your challenge is to write a division and multiplication expression that equal each of the two fractions. The expressions need to use exponents where a fraction is the base of the exponent. For example, if my fraction is $\frac{3}{2}$, one of my expressions might be $\left(\frac{3}{2}\right)^3 \times \left(\frac{2}{3}\right)^2$. The exponent can be 1.

NAME: ______________________ DATE: ______________

LESSON 3.1

Expression Brainstorm Sheet

Directions: Write your one-, two-, three-, and four-digit numbers in the correct area and brainstorm different ways to write them using exponents.

One-digit: ____________	**Two-digit:** ____________
Three-digit: ____________	**Four-digit:** ____________

NAME:______________________________ DATE:______________

LESSON 3.1 PRACTICE

Exponential Expressions

Directions: Complete the problems below.

1. Connolly traced her family history back to three brothers who immigrated to the United States in 1802.
   a. Write an exponential expression that represents the three brothers.

   b. If each of the three brothers married and had three children each, how many children are part of this next generation?

   c. Write a multiplication expression and an exponential expression to represent the three children.

   d. If each child in each generation has three children, how many children will the fifth generation of the family have? Assume that the three brothers are the first generation and their children are the second generation.

2. Two different elementary schools had established phone trees to contact the parents of the school. At Highland Elementary, the lead parent contacts two parents who, in turn, contact two parents each. Each parent who receives a call is responsible for contacting two parents. Lowland Elementary's phone tree asks parents to call five parents at a time. The lead parent at Lowland Elementary calls five parents who then call five parents each and so on.

   a. During the fourth round of calls at Highland Elementary, how many people were called?

   b. How many people were called during the third round of calls at Lowland Elementary?

   c. If 128 parents received calls during the final round of calls at Highland Elementary, how many total parents are involved in the school (remember that one parent starts the phone tree)?

   d. It usually takes the Lowland Elementary parents 30 minutes to complete their five calls. Highland Elementary parents take 10 minutes to complete their calls. If Lowland Elementary's last round of calls involves 125 parents calling 625 parents, how much faster does Highland Elementary finish its phone tree than Lowland Elementary?

Extend Your Thinking

1. Write multiplication and division expressions using only fractions that have exponents. You should try to represent certain integers and fractions using exponential expressions. If you come up with a way to represent a number, rewrite the expression with different fractions that creates the same number. For example, you might represent the number 4 with $\left(\frac{6}{10}\right)^2 \times \left(\frac{10}{3}\right)^2$. Another way to write this would be $\left(\frac{3}{5}\right)^2 \times \left(\frac{20}{6}\right)^2$. You might notice a pattern between the fractions as you come up with your expressions.

Expressions and Equations

NAME:______________________________ DATE:______________

LESSON 3.1

Common Core Assessment Practice

Directions: Complete the problems below.

1. What is the value of three to the fourth power?
   - **a.** 12
   - **b.** 64
   - **c.** 81
   - **d.** 243

2. The number 625 can be written as 5^4. Using the expanded exponential form of 5^4, what is another way to write 625 using an exponential expression?
   - **a.** 25^2
   - **b.** 125^2
   - **c.** 5^3+5^1
   - **d.** 625^0

3. Jose was part of a phone tree for a political campaign. People in the phone tree were responsible for calling 6 people, 4 prospective voters and 2 other campaign callers. When Jose was called to begin his part of the phone tree, he was one of 16 campaign workers called during that part of the calling tree. How many prospective voters will the group of campaign workers that Jose's group called get in touch with?
   - **a.** 32
   - **b.** 64
   - **c.** 128
   - **d.** 256

4. Dr. Jim was studying cell division in his lab at State University. He noticed that the cells he was studying split every 15 minutes. If Dr. Jim started with 5 cells, how many did he have after an hour and a half?
   - **a.** 40
   - **b.** 80
   - **c.** 160
   - **d.** 320

5. The half-life of an unstable atom is measured by the time it takes for an element to lose half of the atomic mass it has at the beginning of the decay. After a period of time, an element now only has 6.25% of its original mass. Write an exponential expression with a fractional base to represent the decay from the original element.

a. $\left(\frac{1}{4}\right)^2$

b. $\left(\frac{1}{2}\right)^4$

c. $\left(\frac{1}{4}\right)^4$

d. $\left(\frac{1}{2}\right)^3$

LESSON 3.2

Equivalent Expressions, Part I

Common Core State Standards

- 6.EE.A.2c
- 6.EE.A.4

Mathematical Practices

- 1, 2, 3, 4, and 6

Estimated Time

- 60–90 minutes

Key Terms

- Expression
- Equivalent
- Variable

Materials

- Lesson 3.2 Activity: Chess and Expressions
- Lesson 3.2 Chessboard Handout
- Lesson 3.2 Chessboard Game Tracker
- Lesson 3.2 Practice: Practice With Equivalent Expressions
- Lesson 3.2 Common Core Assessment Practice

Objectives

In this lesson, students will:

- apply the properties of operations to generate equivalent expressions,
- identify when two expressions are equivalent, and
- evaluate expressions based on a value for the variable.

Lesson 3.2 Activity: Chess and Expressions

Students will begin the lesson by playing a game of chess. Each square corresponds with a different equation. In order for a student to be able to move a piece, he or she must use one of the properties of operations to write an equivalent expression to the one on the square. Both players will then write the equivalent expression on their Lesson 3.2 Chessboard Game Tracker worksheet as well as the operational property that was used. If a player wants to take a piece, his or her opponent may challenge the take by asking the player to solve the expression and giving the player a value for the variable(s) in the expression. Encourage students to use fractions and decimals for the variable values.

For example, during the game of chess, Student 1 moves to capture one of his opponent's pieces. The expression on the square is $15x+25$. Student 1 says that he will use the distributive property to factor out a 5 and rewrite the expression as $5(3x+5)$. While capturing the piece, his opponent, Student 2, challenges Student 1 by asking him to solve the expression if x is equal to $\frac{4}{5}$. The game would continue until one student wins the game.

Teacher's Note. If your students don't know how to play chess, this activity can be adapted easily to checkers instead.

NAME:________________________________ DATE:______________

LESSON 3.2 ACTIVITY

Chess and Expressions

Directions: So, you think you are a chess grandmaster? No? Well, isn't chess your favorite game to play in your free time? Not always? Well, I know that you are a bright student who enjoys creativity and strategy, so this activity is for you!

1. The game starts as a simple game of chess but with one added wrinkle. Moves have to be made with equivalent expressions.
2. Set up the board for a normal game of chess. Begin the game with your partner.
3. When you move to a space, you have to write an expression that is then assigned to that space on the board.
4. Any time another piece is moved to that space (by you or your partner), the person moving the piece has to write an expression equivalent to the expression assigned to that game space. These equivalent expressions are kept on Lesson 3.2 Chessboard Handout and the Lesson 3.2 Chessboard Game Tracker worksheet.
5. If a player is moving to capture one of the other player's pieces, a challenge may be issued on the capture. The player whose piece is being taken can give a value to the attacking player. The attacking player must use that value to solve the equivalent expression that the defending player uses. The variable value must be positive and less than 100.
6. If the attacking player correctly solves the expression, he or she captures the piece. If he or she does not correctly solve the problem, then the piece cannot be captured.
7. Players should track the moves on their Lesson 3.2 Chessboard Handout.

Extend Your Thinking

1. Review each of the expressions that you used during your game. Substitute a fraction or decimal for the variable in each expression and calculate the answers.
2. Change the constants and coefficients in each expression to fractions or decimals. Go through at least five of the new expressions and try to write equivalent expressions. Do you notice any changes from the equivalent expression you wrote to the original expression on the board?

NAME:____ DATE:__________________

LESSON 3.2

Chessboard Handout

Directions: During your game, write the original expression on the blank chessboard below in the square that corresponds to the square on the Lesson 3.2 Chessboard Game Tracker worksheet. Make sure the expression matches the correct space on your game board. As you and your partner move to these spaces, write equivalent expressions below the original one. Keep track of your moves on the chessboard and the Lesson 3.2 Chessboard Game Tracker worksheet. You may need to be aware of how much room is in each space as you are writing.

8								
7								
6								
5								
4								
3								
2								
1								
	A	B	C	D	E	F	G	H

A3: $15+3y+8x+12-2x+9y$

A4: $12+4y+8y-8+7x+14x$

A5: $5\times56+8\times85+13+26$

A6: $9\times24+4\times36+5(60+5)$

B3: $15+23+45+37+12+38$

B4: $32+11+37+28+13+19$

B5: $29+4y+9x+11+8y+3x$

B6: $49+152+28+17+83+21$

C3: $6\times152+8\times213+9\times139$

C4: $2\times149+3\times140+8(20+9)$

C5: $4(12+8)+5(35-5)+9(81-1)$

C6: $5y+8x+15y+12x+30$

D3: $15\times5+32\times15+42\times15$

D4: $12+77+92+36+33$

D5: $12y+8x+9y+16x+15y+4x$

D6: $6(92-2)+3(65+5)+30$

E3: $12+19+17+31+58+93$

E4: $6\times56+8\times48+9\times71$

E5: $34+19+17+38+15+30$

E6: $8+28+24+14+7+21$

F3: $16x+14y+15z+21+60+24$

F4: $44g+72h+90f+11+30+12$

F5: $7\times87+2\times129+4\times99$

F6: $9\times141+12\times139+25\times38$

G3: $8(34-4)+3(143-3)+2(39-9)$

G4: $15+19+149+245+111+241$

G5: $131+78+113+72+19+37$

G6: $91+37+45+55+63+9$

H3: $25x+35y+85z+55+15$

H4: $18+24+36+60x+66y+6z$

H5: $8\times81+9\times91+7\times79$

H6: $4\times201+5\times301+6\times401$

NAME:____________________ DATE:__________

LESSON 3.2
Chessboard Game Tracker Worksheet

Directions: Keep track of your equivalent expressions on the worksheet below. Each line represents a square on the chessboard.

A3: $15+3y+8x+12-2x+9y$ **1.** **2.**	**3.** **4.**
A4: $12+4y+8y-8+7x+14x$ **1.** **2.**	**3.** **4.**
A5: $5\times56+8\times85+13+26$ **1.** **2.**	**3.** **4.**
A6: $9\times24+4\times36+5(60+5)$ **1.** **2.**	**3.** **4.**
B3: $15+23+45+37+12+38$ **1.** **2.**	**3.** **4.**
B4: $32+11+37+28+13+19$ **1.** **2.**	**3.** **4.**

B5: $29+4y+9x+11+8y+3x$ **1.** **2.**	 **3.** **4.**
B6: $49+152+28+17+83+21$ **1.** **2.**	 **3.** **4.**
C3: $6\times152+8\times213+9\times139$ **1.** **2.**	 **3.** **4.**
C4: $2\times149+3\times140+8(20+9)$ **1.** **2.**	 **3.** **4.**
C5: $4(12+8)+5(35-5)+9(81-1)$ **1.** **2.**	 **3.** **4.**
C6: $5y+8x+15y+12x+30$ **1.** **2.**	 **3.** **4.**
D3: $15\times5+32\times15+42\times15$ **1.** **2.**	 **3.** **4.**
D4: $12+77+92+36+33$ **1.** **2.**	 **3.** **4.**

D5: $12y+8x+9y+16x+15y+4x$ **1.** **2.**	**3.** **4.**
D6: $6(92-2)+3(65+5)+30$ **1.** **2.**	**3.** **4.**
E3: $12+19+17+31+58+93$ **1.** **2.**	**3.** **4.**
E4: $6\times56+8\times48+9\times71$ **1.** **2.**	**3.** **4.**
E5: $34+19+17+38+15+30$ **1.** **2.**	**3.** **4.**
E6: $8+28+24+14+7+21$ **1.** **2.**	**3.** **4.**
F3: $16x+14y+15z+21+60+24$ **1.** **2.**	**3.** **4.**
F4: $44g+72h+90f+11+30+12$ **1.** **2.**	**3.** **4.**

F5: $7\times87+2\times129+4\times99$ **1.** **2.**	**3.** **4.**
F6: $9\times141+12\times139+25\times38$ **1.** **2.**	**3.** **4.**
G3: $8(34-4)+3(143-3)+2(39-9)$ **1.** **2.**	**3.** **4.**
G4: $15+19+149+245+111+241$ **1.** **2.**	**3.** **4.**
G5: $131+78+113+72+19+37$ **1.** **2.**	**3.** **4.**
G6: $91+37+45+55+63+9$ **1.** **2.**	**3.** **4.**
H3: $25x+35y+85z+55+15$ **1.** **2.**	**3.** **4.**
H4: $18+24+36+60x+66y+6z$ **1.** **2.**	**3.** **4.**

H5: $8\times81+9\times91+7\times79$	
1.	**3.**
2.	**4.**
H6: $4\times201+5\times301+6\times401$	
1.	**3.**
2.	**4.**

Expressions and Equations

NAME:______________________________ DATE:______________

LESSON 3.2 PRACTICE

Practice With Equivalent Expressions

Directions: Complete the problems below.

1. Sabrina's father wrote an expression to calculate the total amount of money the family makes in a month after the bills are paid. The expression looked like this:

$$6x+4y-3x-2y+1200-800$$

   a. Sabrina realized she could write a much simpler expression that would be equivalent to her father's. What equation could she have written?

   b. If $x = \$500$ and $y = \$300$, how much money does Sabrina's family make every month after bills?

   c. Her father wrote separate expressions for months where there were special expenditures. For example, his expression for June had to account for 5 camps that Sabrina and her siblings attended. If each camp were the same amount, what would his expression have looked like for the month of June?

   d. If Sabrina's family only made $2,200 in June, how much did each camp cost?

2. A local beachfront store sells shoes and T-shirts. The owner, Maggie, is trying to write a simple expression to represent the money she makes each day.
   a. If she sells shoes for \$40 and T-shirts for \$20 and it costs \$100 a day to open her store, what expression could she write to represent her earnings?
   b. How could she rewrite this expression using the distributive property?
   c. If Maggie decided to have a 10% off sale, how would the expression change for the day?
   d. During a normal sales day, Maggie normally sells 12 pairs of shoes and 20 T-shirts. During her 10% off sale, how many shoes and T-shirts does she need to sell to make as much money as she does on a normal day?

Extend Your Thinking

1. Find the squares that were not used or were least used during the chess game and write each one using the three main properties of operations. If you finish early, you and your partner can take turns writing equivalent variations of the expressions and see who can come up with the most.

NAME:______________________________ DATE:______________

LESSON 3.2

Common Core Assessment Practice

Directions: Complete the problems below.

1. Using properties of operations such as the associative, commutative, and distributive properties, what is another way to write the variable expression $8x+5y-2x$?
   - a. $5(x+y+z)$
   - b. $6x+5y$
   - c. $11(x+y)$
   - d. $2(4x+2y-x)$

2. Bronson determined that the money that each of his vending machines earned him per day could be expressed as $6x+11$. If he has 5 vending machines throughout a building, what expression could be used to represent the total money Bronson earns from the building in one day?
   - a. $30x+55$
   - b. $30x+11$
   - c. $11x+16$
   - d. $6x+55$

3. A produce store sells bags of peanuts. Each bag costs $0.35 and then it is an additional $0.15 for every pound of peanuts. If Lucy buys 3 bags and fills each bag with 2 pounds of peanuts, how much money will she have to pay?
   - a. $0.65
   - b. $1.05
   - c. $1.95
   - d. $2.05

4. A fair charges $5 per entry and an additional $0.25 for every booth that a person visits. Jacqueline pays $8.75 after her visit to the fair. How many booths did she visit?
   - a. 15
   - b. 20
   - c. 25
   - d. 30

5. An alarm company is installing an alarm at Collin's house. The company charges $25 for the service visit, $2.50 for every window secured, and $3.75 for every door secured. If *w* represents the number of windows and *d* represents the number of doors, which of the following expressions represents the total cost of the visit?

   a. $25d + 6.25w$

   b. $31.25(d + w)$

   c. $2.50w + 3.75d + 25$

   d. $2.50d + 3.75w + 25$

LESSON 3.3

Equivalent Expressions, Part II

Common Core State Standards

- 6.EE.A.2a
- 6.EE.A.2b
- 6.EE.A.3

Mathematical Practices

- 1, 2, 6, 7, and 8

Estimated Time

- 60–90 minutes

Key Terms

- Expression
- Equivalent
- Variable

Materials

- Lesson 3.3 Activity: Secret Codes With Equivalent Expressions
- Lesson 3.3 Code Creator
- Lesson 3.3 Journal Log
- Lesson 3.3 Practice: Working With Equivalent Expressions
- Lesson 3.3 Common Core Assessment Practice
- Index cards
- Construction paper for making parchment (optional)
- Interactive Underground Railroad (http://teacher.scholastic.com/activities/bhistory/underground_railroad/index.htm)

Objectives

In this lesson, students will:

- apply the properties of operations to generate equivalent expressions,
- identify when two expressions are equivalent, and
- evaluate expressions based on a value for the variable.

Lesson 3.3 Activity: Secret Codes With Equivalent Expressions

The Underground Railroad is well known as a passage that slaves undertook to escape from their life of slavery. The Underground Railroad was not a single route navigated by a single person.

It was a complicated system that involved coordination between the conductors, slaves, and safe houses along the way. Secrecy was a vital part of the success of the Underground Railroad because if information fell to the wrong person it could doom numerous slaves trying to escape.

This lesson will play on that secrecy, albeit a fictitious version of that secrecy. Have students work through the interactive Underground Railroad site provided by Scholastic (http://teacher.scholastic.com/activities/bhistory/underground_railroad/index.htm). This will give them a brief but good background into the Underground Railroad. You are welcome to use materials you already have on the Underground Railroad. This website is simply a suggestion.

In groups, students will develop a series of coded expressions designed to give information to slaves and conductors traveling to the North. Students should design an expression to represent key words that a slave or conductor might need to know during their travels. Keep in mind that speed was paramount so messages had to be brief and easily interpreted by those who understood the code. For example, cardinal directions (north, south, east, and west) might be part of the code system to indicate directions. The coded expression for north could be $3x+15$. If someone wanted to leave that direction to a slave or conductor, he or she would write an expression that is equivalent to the expression for north, such as $3(x+5)$. It was important that the right people interpret the messages, so the expressions have to look different even though they are equivalent.

In this activity, students will come up with key words for the fictitious passage to the North. Students will then assign an expression to each of the words to indicate the key to solving the code. Students will use that code to create secret message cards by writing equivalent expressions to the expressions assigned to the key words. For example, one message might be to alert runaway slaves about food to the west. If the expression for food is $5x+2$ and the expression for west is $2x+20$, students might make a card that reads $2+5x+2(x+10)$ to indicate "food: west." Students can write these messages on paper or construction paper. You can even use tan or lighter colored construction paper to make parchment for the messages.

Students can then post those key words around the school, creating a pseudo-passage to freedom. Students can think of four checkpoints throughout the school and post messages at each checkpoint. The messages should take the other groups (acting as runaway slaves and conductors) through the entire journey to safety by indicating directions to the next checkpoint. Students in the other groups can then find their way to safety by interpreting the coded messages and making the correct choices along the path to reach their goal. The teacher may want to time each group to see who can do it the fastest.

NAME:______________________________ DATE:______________

LESSON 3.3 ACTIVITY

Secret Codes With Equivalent Expressions

Directions: The Underground Railroad is well known as a passage that slaves undertook to escape from their life of slavery. The Underground Railroad was not a single route navigated by a single person. It was a complicated system that involved coordination between the conductors, slaves, and safe houses along the way. Secrecy was a vital part of the success of the Underground Railroad because if information fell to the wrong person it could doom numerous slaves trying to escape.

With your group, you will balance the roles of conductor and safe houses to try to lead a group of slaves to their freedom. An integral part to the Underground Railroad was a method of communicating between the conductors and safe houses that couldn't be easily interpreted by the groups trying to find the escaped slaves. You will be responsible for devising a message that can only be interpreted by those for whom the message is intended.

1. Explore the interactive Underground Railroad at Scholastic.com (http://teacher.scholastic.com/activities/bhistory/underground_railroad/index.htm).

2. With your class, brainstorm different signals/messages that escaping slaves and conductors might need in order to safely find their freedom. For example, there might need to be a message to indicate a location for food and water along their escape route. What other examples do you think might have been useful to the escaping slaves?

3. After you have brainstormed the different messages, assign a variable expression to each of them. The variable expressions can be simple or more complicated. For example, you can do something as simple as $x+5$ and use the commutative property to write an equivalent expression of $5+x$, or the expression may be more complication, such as $5x+4+30+12y$. You can be more creative with their equivalent expressions if the expressions are more complicated. Use Lesson 3.3 Code Creator to help you.

4. Begin devising a series of messages that you would leave along a trail to a group of escaping slaves. These messages should be equivalent to the expressions that you assigned above but look different. Use the associative, commutative, and distributive properties to manipulate the expressions while still keeping them equivalent to the assigned expression. For example, you might decide you need a code to indicate "danger ahead." The expression could be $2x+7$. Using the commutative property, the equivalent expression would be $7+2x$. Write your messages on the index cards provided.

5. After you have your messages completed and placed onto index cards (or construction paper), design a path throughout your school that other groups might follow to "freedom." Establish checkpoints to which real runaway slaves may have traveled. Your messages should lead the other groups between checkpoints to the final checkpoint (safety). The other groups will keep a journal entry as they go through each direction and indicate how they interpreted the message and what the next step in their journey might be.

6. You will also need to follow another group's path to freedom and keep a journal of your travels on Lesson 3.3 Journal Log. As you come to an index card or construction paper message, interpret the equivalent expression and find the hidden message that it represents. Keep track of your decisions as you move from message to message.

Extend Your Thinking

1. One point over which some historians disagree is the manner in which the messages were communicated throughout the journey. It has long been speculated that hidden messages were woven into quilts, but the evidence hasn't been definitive enough to say for certain. Assuming that messages were actually hidden in quilts, create a quilt (using construction paper) that contains numerous expressions, only some of which actually contain the message. Within the extraneous expressions, hide the equivalent expressions that contain the message. Put the quilt together with different colors and designs and see if the other groups in your class can identify the message that you intended.

2. On another piece of paper, write a letter from a conductor requesting assistance of a safe house. With a partner, get into character of a conductor and pretend to be writing from his or her perspective. Incorporate details into your letter that are specific to the hardships of the journey. Inside the body of the letter, create a coded message that contains the necessary information using equivalent expressions. Try to naturally incorporate the equivalent expressions into the letter as they might appear in mathematical word problems that you have done in class.

3. When people joined the Underground Railroad, they had to be taught how the code works. Pretend you are preparing a group of slaves for the arduous journey north. Create a tutorial that explains to the slaves how to manipulate the basic expression of the code into a more complicated, equivalent expression that can elude the authorities. Give them examples of specific code words/phrases and the types of equivalent expressions that they might see throughout their journey. Keep in mind that it was illegal to educate slaves, so your tutorial needs to be designed for someone who may not have seen these types of code before.

NAME:______________________________ DATE:______________

LESSON 3.3

Code Creator

Directions: On this sheet, decide what messages you would like to convey to the travelers of the Underground Railroad. Create a coded expression for each one and then brainstorm a few different ways to write equivalent expressions for each one.

1. **Key Word to Travelers:** ______________________________

   Coded Expression to Represent this Key Word: ______________________________

   Possible Equivalent Expressions:

2. **Key Word to Travelers:** ______________________________

   Coded Expression to Represent this Key Word: ______________________________

   Possible Equivalent Expressions:

3. **Key Word to Travelers:** ______________________________

   Coded Expression to Represent this Key Word: ______________________________

   Possible Equivalent Expressions:

NAME:____________________ DATE:__________

LESSON 3.3

Journal Log

Directions: Create fictional journal entries to document your journey through the Underground Railroad as you follow the clues that your classmates have left for you. Try to think of conflicts that the real travelers of the Underground Railroad had to face along their arduous journeys to freedom.

Beginning of Your Journey

Checkpoint 1

1. Coded message: ____________________

2. Meaning behind the message:

Checkpoint 2

1. Coded message: ____________________

2. Meaning behind the message:

Checkpoint 3

1. Coded message: ____________________

2. Meaning behind the message:

Checkpoint 4

1. Coded message: ____________________

2. Meaning behind the message:

LESSON 3.3 PRACTICE

Working With Equivalent Expressions

Directions: Complete the problems below.

1. Jessica's teacher gives her the expression $9b-12c+15b$ and asks her to simplify the expression.
   a. Jessica's first step is to rewrite the expression as $9b+15b-12c$. What operational property did Jessica use to change the equation?

   b. Explain the most logical next step to simplifying this expression after Jessica rewrites the expression as shown in Part A.

   c. Jessica decides that her last step in simplifying the equation is to use the distributive property. Looking at both of the coefficients, Jessica notices that both numbers share a common factor of 3, and she writes the final expression as $3(8b-4c)$. Is this the simplest way to write the expression? If not, explain how she could have done it differently.

   d. One of Jessica's classmates, Blaine, told Jessica that all he did was add 9 and 15 and then subtract 12 to get a final answer of $12c$. Jessica explains to Blaine that he cannot combine coefficients of different variables. Write out what her explanation could have been.

2. A school was ordering graduation outfits for its fifth-grade students. Each outfit for the boys was \$24, and each outfit for the girls was \$36 dollars.
   a. If b represents the number of boys in the fifth grade, and g represents the number of girls in the fifth grade, write a variable expression to represent this problem.

   b. A parent who was in charge of ordering the outfits realized that she could use the distributive property to make her calculations go much more quickly. How did she rewrite the expression?

   c. If there are 12 boys in the fifth grade and 20 girls in the fifth grade, by what number would the parent multiply 12 to find out the total cost of the outfits?

   d. How much do the outfits cost all together?

Extend Your Thinking

1. Create an interactive PowerPoint slide show that functions similarly to a choose-your-own-adventure story. You will create a brief story on the slides and offer choices. Each part of your story should contain an expression or a word problem that contains an expression. You will have to use your knowledge of equivalent expressions to make the correct decision. The correct decision will be the decision that is an equivalent expression to the expression in that part of the story. All other expressions should not be equivalent and would be the incorrect decision. The correct decision will take you to the next step of the journey.

NAME:________________________ DATE:____________

LESSON 3.3

Common Core Assessment Practice

Directions: Complete the problems below.

1. What is another way to write the expression $15x+45$?
   a. $60x$
   b. 30
   c. $15(x+30)$
   d. $15(x+3)$

2. What is the coefficient of x after using the associative property in the expression $32x-12x+18y$?
   a. 38
   b. 20
   c. 26
   d. 32

3. Which operational property would you use to change around the order of the operands in an expression?
   a. Commutative
   b. Associative
   c. Distributive
   d. Alternative

4. Which of the following is equivalent to the expression $4(x+3)-2x$?
   a. $12x+3$
   b. $2(x+3)$
   c. $6(x+6)$
   d. $12(x+6)$

5. Which of the following expressions is equivalent to $17c-9d+c$?
   a. $17c-8d$
   b. $9(2c-9d)$
   c. $3(6c-3d)$
   d. $16c-9d$

LESSON 3.4

Solving Expressions

Common Core State Standards

- 6.EE.B.5
- 6.EE.B.6
- 6.EE.B.7

Mathematical Practices

- 1, 2, 3, 5, 6, 7, and 8

Estimated Time

- 60–90 minutes

Key Terms

- Expression
- Equivalent
- Variable
- Equation

Materials

- Lesson 3.4 Activity: Fantasy Football Expressions
- Lesson 3.4 Draft Board Handout
- Lesson 3.4 Fantasy Point Calculations
- Lesson 3.4 Fantasy Football Simulated Game
- Lesson 3.4 Practice: Solving Equations
- Lesson 3.4 Common Core Assessment Practice
- Six-sided dice

Objectives

In this lesson, students will:

- solve one-step equations in real-world situations.

Lesson 3.4 Activity: Fantasy Football Expressions

Fantasy football is a fun way for students to keep track of their favorite player's statistics during a season. In this lesson, students will conduct a mini draft by selecting professional football players (a quarterback, a wide receiver, and a running back) to construct a team. Students should use the list on Lesson 3.4 Draft Board Handout to make their selections. Students will look at each player's stats from the previous 2 years and calculate the per-game averages for each one of the listed statistical categories. As they play around with the statistics, students will write equations to represent their calculations, and then demonstrate how to solve the equations. To help them with their calculations, students should follow the basic point system provided on the Lesson 3.4 Fantasy Point Calculations worksheet. Using their average statistics, students will then play simulated games, using the dice to calculate the points that their team earns. Students can compare that total to other students or groups in the class to see who wins the fantasy game.

NAME:______________________________ DATE:______________

LESSON 3.4 ACTIVITY

Fantasy Football Expressions

Directions: Who would you choose if you could create a team of your favorite football players? Today we are going to play a game of fantasy football.

1. Your group will draft a quarterback, running back, and wide receiver from Lesson 3.4 Draft Board Handout.
2. Lesson 3.4 Draft Board Handout lists the players and the statistics for that player for 2 years. When you draft the player, write down that player's statistics on your Lesson 3.4 Fantasy Point Calculations worksheet. Do that for every player you draft (a total of 3).
3. There will be a missing statistic for each one of your players. Write an equation that will solve for that missing statistic. When you have solved for the missing statistic, fill it into the table.
4. For each statistic, calculate the average over the 2-year period listed. Use that average to help you simulate your games.
5. After calculating the averages for each of the players and their statistics, your group will play a simulated game by using a six-sided die and completing the Lesson 3.4 Fantasy Football Simulated Game handout. For each position, there is an equation that helps you figure out the player's stats for that game. Roll the die and solve the equations listed on the Lesson 3.4 Fantasy Football Simulated Game handout to figure out the number of yards, touchdowns, and completions that your player had during that simulated game. You will have to substitute the values of your average stats and the die rolls into the equations to solve. Use the fantasy point values to calculate the total number of fantasy points each of your players earned for that simulated game.
6. Solve the equations to figure out the statistics and then calculate the total points for the three players on your team. The group whose players score the highest total of points wins the game.
7. You can then play additional games with the same group or different groups to see how the outcomes differ and to practice writing and solving equations.

Extend Your Thinking

1. Point averages for players will probably have decimal values. During the simulated games, do the calculations during a simulated game using decimal values and converted fractional values. If you have not already written your averages as decimals/fractions, go back to your tables and rewrite the point averages as both a fraction and a decimal. During a simulated game, you should use the fraction and decimal equations to calculate the statistics and fantasy points involved in the game simulation.

2. Research the average statistics for an NFL kicker during a season and how the points for kickers are calculated in fantasy football. With your partner(s) create a table and set of equations on another sheet that would allow the position of kicker to be added into the game. You need to think of how the kicker's points would vary based on the different possible die rolls and adjust your equations so that it is still realistic.

NAME:______________________________ DATE:______________

LESSON 3.4 ACTIVITY

Draft Board Handout

Quarterbacks

Point system: 0.1 point per completion; 1 point every 20 yards; 4 points per touchdown; -2 points per interception. Round all point values to the nearest whole number.

	Completions	Yards	Touchdowns	Interceptions	Points
1. Drew Brees					
2014	456	4,952	33		392
2013	446	5,162	39		436
Avg.					
2. Ben Roethlisberger					
2014	408	4,952	32		399
2013	375	4,261	28		335
Avg.					
3. Andrew Luck					
2014	380	4,761	40		404
2013	343	3,822	23		299
Avg.					
4. Peyton Manning					
2014	395	4,727	39		402
2013	450	5,477	55		519
Avg.					
5. Matt Ryan					
2014	415	4,694	28		361
2013	439	4,515	26		340
Avg.					
6. Eli Manning					
2014	379	4,410	30		351
2013	317	3,818	18		261
Avg.					

	Completions	Yards	Touchdowns	Interceptions	Points
7. Aaron Rodgers					
2014	341	4,381	38		395
2012	371	4,295	39		392
Avg.					
8. Philip Rivers					
2014	379	4,286	31		340
2013	378	4,478	32		368
Avg.					
9. Matthew Stafford					
2014	363	4,257	22		313
2013	446	4,650	29		348
Avg.					
10. Tom Brady					
2014	373	4,109	33		356
2013	380	4,343	25		333
Avg.					
11. Russell Wilson					
2014	285	3,475	20		269
2013	257	3,357	26		280
Avg.					
12.					
13.					
14.					

Running Backs

Point system: 0.1 per attempt; 1 point for every 10 yards; 6 points per touchdown. Round all point values to the nearest whole number.

	Attempts	Yards	Touchdowns	Points
1. DeMarco Murray				
2014	392	1,845		302
2013	217	1,121		188
Avg.				
2. Le'Veon Bell				
2014	290	1,361		213
2013	244	890		161
Avg.				
3. LeSean McCoy				
2014	312	1,319		193
2013	314	1,607		246
Avg.				
4. Marshawn Lynch				
2014	280	1,306		237
2013	301	1,257		228
Avg.				
5. Arian Foster				
2014	260	1,246		199
2012	351	1,424		267
Avg.				
6. Eddie Lacy				
2014	246	1,124		191
2013	284	1,178		212
Avg.				
7. Alfred Morris				
2014	265	1,074		182
2013	276	1,275		198
Avg.				

	Attempts	Yards	Touchdowns	Points
8. Matt Forte				
2014	266	1,038		167
2013	289	1,339		217
Avg.				
9. Jamaal Charles				
2014	206	1,033		178
2013	259	1,287		227
Avg.				
10. Frank Gore				
2014	255	1,106		161
2013	276	1,128		195
Avg.				
11.				
12.				
13.				

Wide Receivers

Point system: 0.1 per reception; 1 point for every 10 yards; 6 points per touchdown. Round all point values to the nearest whole number.

	Receptions	Yards	Touchdowns	Points
1. Antonio Brown				
2014	129	1,698		261
2013	110	1,499		209
Avg.				
2. Demaryius Thomas				
2014	111	1,619		239
2013	92	1,430		236
Avg.				
3. Julio Jones				
2014	104	1,593		205
2012	79	1,198		188
Avg.				
4. Jordy Nelson				
2014	98	1,519		240
2013	85	1,314		188
Avg.				
5. Emmanuel Sanders				
2014	101	1,404		204
2013	67	740		117
Avg.				
6. T.Y. Hilton				
2014	82	1,345		185
2013	82	1,083		146
Avg.				
7. Dez Bryant				
2014	88	1,320		237
2013	93	1,233		210
Avg.				

	Receptions	Yards	Touchdowns	Points
8. Jeremy Maclin				
2014	85	1,318		201
2012	69	857		135
Avg.				
9. Alshon Jeffery				
2014	85	1,133		182
2013	89	1,421		193
Avg.				
10. Calvin Johnson				
2014	71	1,077		163
2013	84	1,492		229
Avg.				
11.				
12.				
13.				

NAME:____ DATE:______________

LESSON 3.4 ACTIVITY

Fantasy Point Calculations

Directions: After you have finished drafting your fantasy players, enter in their stats and complete the following questions about each.

1. Quarterback (QB): ________________________________

	Completions	Yards	Touchdowns	Interceptions	Points
2014					
2013					
Avg.					

a. Determine with your group members how to solve for the number of interceptions that your QB threw in 2014 and 2013 (note that some players may have been injured in 2013 so the 2012 stats were used instead). Write an equation that can be solved for the number of interceptions. Fill in the values in the table above.

Equation: ________________________________

b. Find the averages for each statistical category over the 2 years and write it in the appropriate space above.

c. Using the averages, write a variable equation that would yield the per-game average for each of the statistics. Assume that each player plays 16 games and that the variable in the equation represents the per-game average. Round your answers to the nearest tenth.

	Completions	Yards	Touchdowns	Interceptions	Points
Equation					
Per-game average					

2. Running Back (RB): ______________________________

	Attempts	Yards	Touchdowns	Points
2014				
2013				
Avg.				

a. Determine with your group members how to solve for the number of touchdowns that your RB scored in 2014 and 2013 (note that some players may have been injured in 2013 so the 2012 stats were used instead). Write an equation that can be solved for the number of touchdowns. Fill in the values in the table above.

Equation: ______________________________

b. Find the averages for each statistical category over the 2 years and write it in the appropriate space above.

c. Using the averages, write a variable equation that would yield the per-game average for each of the statistics. Assume that each player plays 16 games and that the variable in the equation represents the per-game average. Round your answers to the nearest tenth.

	Attempts	Yards	Touchdowns	Points
Equation				
Per-game average				

3. Wide Receiver (WR): ______________________________

	Receptions	Yards	Touchdowns	Points
2014				
2013				
Avg.				

a. Determine with your group members how to solve for the number of touchdowns that your WR scored in 2014 and 2013 (note that some players may have been injured in 2013 so the 2012 stats were used instead). Write an equation that can be solved for the number of touchdowns. Fill in the values in the table above.

Equation: ______________________________

b. Find the averages for each statistical category over the 2 years and write it in the appropriate space above.

c. Using the averages, write a variable equation that would yield the per-game average for each of the statistics. Assume that each player plays 16 games and that the variable in the equation represents the per-game average. Round your answers to the nearest tenth.

	Receptions	Yards	Touchdowns	Points
Equation				
Per-game average				

NAME:______________________________ DATE:______________

LESSON 3.4

Fantasy Football Simulated Game

Directions: Use your answers on the Fantasy Point Calculations worksheet to simulate your game. Your group will challenge another group to a fantasy football game. You will need at least one six-sided die for this activity. You will simulate the stats for each of your fantasy players. After the simulation, use the point conversions to change the statistics into fantasy points. You will need to use your per-game averages in your simulation to find the statistics.

FANTASY POINT VALUES: QUARTERBACK

Completions	Yards	Touchdowns	Interceptions
1 point for every 10 completions	1 point for every 20 yards	4 points for every passing touchdown	-2 points for every interception

C = per-game completions; Y = per-game yards; T = per-game touchdowns; I = per-game interceptions; D = dice roll

- Completions: Roll your die. The number of completions in this game is $\frac{C}{D}+20$.
- Yards: Roll your die. The number of yards in this game is $\frac{Y}{D}+150$.
- Touchdowns: Roll your die twice (D1 and D2). The number of touchdowns in this game is $\frac{T}{D1}+D2$. (Round your answer to the nearest whole number.)
- Interceptions: Roll your die. The number of interceptions in this game is $\left(\frac{D}{2}\right)\times I$. (Round your answer to the nearest whole number.)

Quarterback: ______________________________

Completions	Yards	Touchdowns	Interceptions	Fantasy Points

Expressions and Equations

FANTASY POINT VALUES: RUNNING BACK

Attempts 1 point for every 15 attempts	**Yards** 1 point for every 10 yards	**Touchdowns** 6 points for every touchdown

A = per-game attempts; Y = per-game yards; T = per-game touchdowns; D = dice roll

- Attempts: Roll your die. The number of attempts this game is $\frac{A}{D}+12$.
- Yards: Roll your die. The number of yards this game is $\frac{Y}{D}+60$.
- Touchdowns: Roll your die twice (D1 and D2). The number of touchdowns in this game is $\left(\frac{T}{D1}\right)\times D2$. (Round your answer to the nearest whole number.)

Running Back: ______________________________

Attempts	Yards	Touchdowns	Fantasy Points

Expressions and Equations

FANTASY POINT VALUES: WIDE RECEIVER

Receptions 1 point for every 5 receptions	**Yards** 1 point for every 10 yards	**Touchdowns** 6 points for every touchdown

R: per-game receptions; *Y*: per-game yards; *T*: per-game touchdowns; *D*: dice roll

- Receptions: Roll your die. The number of receptions this game is $\left(\frac{4}{D}\right)\times R$.
- Yards: Roll your die. The number of yards this game is $\frac{Y}{D}+60$.
- Touchdowns: Roll your die twice (D1 and D2). The number of touchdowns in this game is $\left(\frac{T}{D1}\right)\times D2$. (Round your answer to the nearest whole number.)

Wide Receiver: ______________________________

Receptions	Yards	Touchdowns	Fantasy Points

NAME:____ DATE:_______________

LESSON 3.4 PRACTICE

Solving Equations

Directions: Complete the problems below.

1. Sergio owns a small appliance store. He is in the process of trying to project his profits over the course of a year to better plan his family's finances. To open his store for a week, it costs him \$350. The first week, his store grossed \$1,154; the second week, his store grossed \$1,232; the third week, his store grossed \$1,079; and the fourth week, his store grossed \$1,105.
   a. How much profit did Sergio earn in each of the first 4 weeks?

   b. Explain how you could use the profits from the first 4 weeks to project the profit for each week that the store is open.

   c. If x represents the number of weeks that the store has been open, write a variable expression to estimate the total profits earned for that number of weeks.

   d. How much profit will Sergio earn during the course of a year (52 weeks)?

Expressions and Equations

e. When Sergio first wrote an expression to solve for his yearly profits, he wrote the expression $1143x - 350$. He took the average of his gross earnings and put that as the coefficient and then subtracted the 350 cost of running his store. Explain why this expression is incorrect.

2. A snack company sells vending machines for $500. Nedal purchases a snack machine, which has a variety of snacks for $2 each.
   a. If s represents the number of snacks sold, write an expression to represent the net amount of money that Nedal has earned from his snack machine.

   b. Determine the net money that Nedal has earned by selling 15 snacks, 50 snacks, and 300 snacks respectively. Indicate whether he has earned a profit or loss.

   c. How many snacks will Nedal have to sell if he wants to break even? Explain how you came to your answer.

d. Nedal's friend, Jenna, decides to purchase 5 snack machines for $500 each. If s represents the number of snacks sold at one snack machine, what expression could be written to represent Jenna's net earnings among all 5 snack machines? Assume each snack machine sells the same number of snacks.

e. Using the distributive property, what is another way to write the expression from Part D?

Extend Your Thinking

1. Going back to the fantasy activity, simulate one game for each of your three players by rolling the dice. Using that information, multiply the per-game totals by 16 and see if it compares to the average stats for each of the three players. After that, simulate four games and find the average stats for those four games. Then multiply the averages for the four games so that they are equivalent to 16 games. Are the averages closer to the four game totals than the one game totals? Explain why.

NAME: ______________________ DATE: ______________

Expressions and Equations

LESSON 3.4

Common Core Assessment Practice

Directions: Complete the problems below.

1. Justin is trying to raise money to buy a bicycle that cost \$198. He offers a lawn service to his neighborhood in order to raise the money. He charges \$15 per lawn. If he has \$50 saved already, how many lawns will he need to mow to raise enough money to buy the bicycle?
   - **a.** 9
   - **b.** 10
   - **c.** 13
   - **d.** 14

2. Amnah earns \$25 for working a day at a cell phone accessory store at the mall. She also earns \$4 for every item that she sells at the store. If a represents the number of accessories that Amnah sells, write an expression to represent the amount of money she earns in a day.
   - **a.** $29a$
   - **b.** $25a + 4$
   - **c.** $4a + 25$
   - **d.** $4a + 25a$

3. Jesse splits his collection of candy between himself and 7 of his friends. If each friend gets 9 pieces of candy, how many pieces of candy did Jesse have originally?
   - **a.** 56
   - **b.** 63
   - **c.** 64
   - **d.** 72

4. At the beginning of the fourth quarter, Union College's basketball team had 50 points. During the fourth quarter, they scored four 3-point field goals and a number of 2-point field goals. If Union College ended the game with 78 points, how many 2-point field goals did they score in the fourth quarter?
   - **a.** 8
   - **b.** 12
   - **c.** 14
   - **d.** 16

5. A valve pumps 2 liters of water out every minute. After 30 minutes, the pump rate doubles. If the valve continues for another hour at the doubled rate, how many liters of water have been pumped altogether?
   a. 60 liters
   b. 90 liters
   c. 180 liters
   d. 300 liters

LESSON 3.5

Inequality Expressions

Common Core State Standards

- 6.EE.B.8

Mathematical Practices

- 1, 2, 3, 4, 5, and 6

Estimated Time

- 60–90 minutes

Key Terms

- Inequality
- Variable
- Constraint
- Condition

Materials

- Lesson 3.5 Activity: Inequalities in Our Lives
- Lesson 3.5 Practice: Working With Inequalities
- Lesson 3.5 Common Core Assessment Practice
- Poster board
- Markers
- Ruler
- Construction paper
- Glue
- Index cards

Objectives

In this lesson, students will:

- write inequality expressions that represent real-world conditions or constraints.

Lesson 3.5 Activity: Inequalities in Our Lives

One of the most recognizable inequalities for students is the sign at amusement parks that indicates the minimum height to ride on the attraction. Students can easily represent this as a variable inequality.

This lesson will be based on this premise of inequalities that we encounter in our everyday lives. The teacher will begin the lesson by showing students an amusement park height sign and asking them to write an inequality based on this sign. Students will then brainstorm other real-world situations that might involve inequalities. Encourage students to be creative with their inequalities and see how many they can come up with as a class.

Students will then create a sign, similar to the amusement park sign, that represents a real-world inequality that they chose to portray. The sign should represent a picture representation of the situation, whether serious or comical, and a corresponding inequality that represents that situation.

NAME: ______________________ DATE: ______________

LESSON 3.5 ACTIVITY

Inequalities in Our Lives

Directions: Do you remember when you were a younger kid and couldn't ride the rides that had height requirements? The signs usually said, "You must be this tall to ride this ride." These are your basic inequalities in math.

1. Look at the example picture that your teacher has provided. Write a basic inequality that represents this sign.

2. Brainstorm different scenarios you might encounter in the real world. Be creative!

3. Choose one of the scenarios and design a sign similar to the amusement park sign using the supplies provided. The sign should show the real-world scenario and have the corresponding inequality written on the sign as well.

Extend Your Thinking

1. Create inequality cards using index cards. The inequality cards should have a variable and the inequality that shows the comparison between the variable and a value. You and your partner(s) will take turns playing one of the inequality cards at a time. When the card is played, your other group members will write down a scenario that they believe best corresponds to that inequality. The person who played the card will then choose the situation that he or she thinks is best and explain why based on the inequality.

2. Represent a sign that has two constraints to it and can be written as an inequality $c > x > d$ where c and d are constants that represent the constraints and x is the variable that falls between the constraints.

NAME:______________________________ DATE:______________

LESSON 3.5 PRACTICE

Working With Inequalities

Directions: Complete the problems below.

1. A special school field trip was planned for all students who raised at least $50 for the School Success Fund.

   a. If *r* represents the amount of money raised by a student, write an inequality to represent the amount of money that needs to be raised in order to attend the field trip.

   b. Kayla wanted to go on the field trip and had already raised $15. She was selling handmade candles in her neighborhood for $2 each. What is the fewest number of candles she would need to sell in order to make the field trip? Write an inequality and solve.

   c. The reward setup for the fund raiser indicated that any student who had sold at least $50 but less than $150 would be eligible for the field trip but not for the grand prize drawing. Write this as an inequality. Let *r* represent the amount of money raised.

d. Adeline was selling handcrafted jewelry for the fund raiser. She had already qualified for the field trip but really wanted to be entered into the grand prize drawing. Each piece of jewelry sells for $7. What is the maximum number of pieces of jewelry that she would need to sell in order to be entered into the drawing? Write an inequality and solve. Assume that Adeline's fund-raising has only come from selling jewelry.

2. Caleb is trying to get one of his cold drinks to be as cold as possible. He figures that every minute he leaves the cold drink in the freezer, the temperature of the drink drops 2 degrees Fahrenheit.
   a. If the cold drink starts out at a temperature of 75 degrees Fahrenheit, what is the maximum amount of time the Caleb can leave his drink in the freezer before it freezes? Assume that 32 degrees Fahrenheit is freezing temperature.

   b. Caleb's friend, Zachary, wants to do the same thing. He leaves his cold drink in the freezer for 30 minutes, but when he takes it out of the freezer it is frozen. What is the maximum temperature that the cold drink could have been before Zachary placed it in the freezer? Write an inequality and solve.

Extend Your Thinking

1. Think of everyday activities in your life and try to turn them into inequalities. For example, you may have a set amount of TV time that can be written as an inequality. You should make a chart of activities that happen to you throughout your day and represent these activities using inequalities.

NAME: ______________________________ DATE: ______________

LESSON 3.5

Common Core Assessment Practice

Directions: Complete the problems below.

1. In order to pass his history class, Philip must score at least an 80% on his final exam. Write this as an inequality. Let *s* indicate his final exam score.
   a. $s \geq 80$
   b. $s > 80$
   c. $s \leq 80$
   d. $s < 80$

2. A store sells pencils for $0.10 each. On one day, the store has earned $585. What is the minimum number of pencils the store has to sell in order to earn at least $600 for the day?
   a. 2 pencils
   b. 15 pencils
   c. 150 pencils
   d. 200 pencils

3. Sayer dives for golf balls at his local course and sells them to golfers. He makes $15 for a bag of 100 golf balls. If he is saving to buy a $190 necklace for his mother, how many golf balls does he need to find in order to earn enough money?
   a. 14
   b. 15
   c. 1,200
   d. 1,300

4. Sydney opened up a kiosk at the mall that sells science fiction memorabilia. She sells each piece of memorabilia for $30. If it cost Sydney $800 to open the kiosk, write an inequality to represent the number of pieces of memorabilia that she would have to sell in order to break even. Let *m* represent the pieces of memorabilia that Sydney sells.
   a. $30m \geq 0$
   b. $30m \leq 0$
   c. $30m \geq 800$
   d. $30m + 800 \geq 0$

5. Ryanne missed a penalty kick in her last soccer game. As punishment, her coach made her kick 15 sets of penalty kicks before she could leave practice. Each set is 10 kicks. If she has currently kicked 28 penalty kicks, how many more sets does she have to complete before she can leave practice?
   a. 12
   b. 13
   c. 14
   d. 15

LESSON 3.6

Independent and Dependent Variables

Common Core State Standards

- 6.EE.B.9

Mathematical Practices

- 1, 2, 4, 5, 6

Estimated Time

- 60–90 minutes

Key Terms

- Expression
- Independent variable
- Dependent variable

Materials

- Lesson 3.6 Activity: Variables in Flight
- Lesson 3.6 Flight Tracking Worksheet
- Lesson 3.6 Practice: Working With Independent and Dependent Variables
- Lesson 3.6 Common Core Assessment Practice
- Flightaware (http://flightaware.com)
- Freemaptools (http://freemaptools.com)

Objectives

In this lesson, students will:

- represent and analyze the relationship between an independent and dependent variable, specifically distance and time.

Lesson 3.6 Activity: Variables in Flight

Students will begin the lesson by choosing a starting location and a destination to which they will fly. Emphasize that a direct flight will make the activity much more manageable. Students will use Flightaware to search their flight route(s) and look at the specifics of each flight, specifically the distance of the flight and the time it took to reach the destination.

Begin the activity by having students calculate the average rate of speed using distance and time. Students will use this rate when looking at the relationship between the time that a flight has been in the air and its distance. The activity will involve students figuring out distances at specific times during a flight and comparing them to the actual flight tracker of a plane that is currently in the air.

Students will also pick out well-known cities that fall within the path of the flight. Students will use the distance between that city and the starting location using a map application (Freemaptools is a good place to visit) to hypothesize the time it will take for the flight to get there. Students will keep track of these calculations on a table and graph and use this information when tracking a live flight. Students can then compare their fight to other flights that have traveled between the two cities and discuss reasons why the flight duration might be different.

NAME:______________________________ DATE:______________

LESSON 3.6 ACTIVITY

Variables in Flight

Directions: Have you ever flown on an airplane? If you have, chances are you have looked out the window and seen a sprawling countryside or a city in the distance. Have you ever looked outside the plane and wondered exactly where you were? In this activity, you will be able to estimate your location on a plane based on the time you have been flying.

1. Choose two cities within the United States between which you would like to fly. Try to choose two cities that might have a direct flight between them.

2. Use Flightaware (http://flightaware.com) to search for all flights that travel between the two cities that you chose. The website will give you a bunch of information about each of the flights.

3. Choose five flights that have already completed their trips and look at the distance each flight traveled and the time in which it took to reach its destination.

4. Using the formula $d = rt$, calculate the rate (average speed) of each of the five flights. Find the average rate of all of the five flights. This average rate will be used in making predictions on future flights.

5. Using the average rate, fill in the table on Lesson 3.6 Flight Tracking Worksheet indicating how far the plane has traveled at given times (every 15–20 minutes is a good interval).

6. Graph the table on the graph provided on Lesson 3.6 Flight Tracking Worksheet.

7. Open up Flightaware and look for a flight that is en route. When you click on the flight, it will give you a time that the plane has been flying. Plug that time in using your average rate and calculate a distance. Check that distance against the current distance that is listed on the flight tracker.

8. Look at the route that your flight takes between the cities that you chose. Choose cities/landmarks in between the two cities that the flight path goes through (or pretty near). Using a map application (http://freemaptools.com), find the distance between each of the cities that you picked and the starting location. Calculate the time that you think it will take the average flight to pass over each of the cities in between. Compare your calculations to your observations as you track your flight.

9. Write a brief explanation about why the flight times might be different even though the planes are all traveling between the same two cities.

Extend Your Thinking

1. Look a bit more carefully at the flights between the two cities that you chose. Look at flights that use different types of airplanes. Some of the flights may use a larger plane while others might use a smaller plane. Compare the average rate of speed between these planes. Make a table for both types of planes (or as many different types as you'd like). Graph both of the tables and compare them. What do you notice about the two graphs as it might relate to the types of planes you are comparing?

2. A tailwind is a wind behind the plane that usually increases the plane's speed. A headwind is a wind into which the plane is flying and usually decreases the plane's speed. In fact, the speed of a tailwind can be added directly into the average rate of speed of the plane while a headwind will be subtracted from the average speed of the plane. Experiment with a 15 mph tailwind and 15 mph headwind. Adjust the average speed accordingly and see how it affects the time it would take to reach certain places along the flight path and ultimately the final destination. Write a conclusion about how the tailwind and headwind affect the overall time of the trip. Use your calculations in your answer. Hint: Look to see if the time differences are constant.

NAME:______________________________ DATE:______________

LESSON 3.6

Flight Tracking Worksheet

Directions: Use Flightaware.com and Freemaptools.com to help you complete this activity.

Choose a city in the United States: ______________________________

From that city, choose a travel destination: ______________________________

1. Using Flightaware.com, write down the distance and duration of the previous five flights between the two cities above.

	Flight 1	Flight 2	Flight 3	Flight 4	Flight 5	Average
Distance						
Duration						

2. Use the formula $d = rt$ to calculate the average rate of speed of the planes on this route.

   Average rate of speed: ______________________________

3. Compare your average rate of speed to the actual average rate of speed listed on Flightaware.com. Brainstorm and explain why there might be some differences.

4. Look at Flightaware.com and find a flight that is currently flying between your two cities. Look at the time that it has been in the air and use that time and your average rate to estimate the distance traveled.

a. Does it match the actual distance of the flight?

b. Look at the route and determine what might have caused a discrepancy. Explain.

5. Look over the route that planes fly between your two cities and find three major cities/landmarks that the plane will fly over or near. Use Freemaptools.com to determine the distance between your starting location and each of the three cities. Using your average speed, estimate the time it would take for the plane to reach the locations.

Location	Distance	Estimated Time

NAME:______________________________ DATE:______________

LESSON 3.6 PRACTICE

Working With Independent and Dependent Variables

Directions: Complete the problems below.

1. A train is traveling along the Pacific coastline stopping occasionally to drop off and pick up passengers. The train moves at a speed of 45 mph.
   a. Write an equation to represent a train's distance based on its rate and time.

   b. Complete a table to indicate the distance that the train has traveled at specific times. Remember that the rate is in miles per hour.

Time (minutes)	Distance (miles)
30 minutes	
60 minutes	
120 minutes	
150 minutes	
240 minutes	
255 minutes	

   c. The train leaves the station at San Franco. The train stops at Pattersonville for 20 minutes and then continues to its next main stop at Sierra Verde. If the total time it took the train to get from San Franco to Sierra Verde was 160 minutes, how far away is San Franco from Sierra Verde?

d. A train travels 144 miles during its trip. If the train had two 10-minute stops during the trip, how long did the trip take in total? Your answer should be written in hours and minutes.

2. Rhys runs an orange farm. She plants the orange trees in rows of 10. Each tree yields, on average, 80 oranges in a season.
   a. Write two equations that represent the total oranges yielded on her farm during a season. One equation should be based on the total number of trees, and the second equation should be based on the number of rows.

   b. Complete a table to represent the total number of oranges based on the number of rows of trees.

Rows	Oranges
3 rows	
6 rows	
8 rows	
10.5 rows	
12 rows	
20 rows	

c. Rhys originally has 30 rows of orange trees on her farm. She clears some land and decides to plant 16 and a half new rows. If she sells a dozen oranges for $5.50, how much money can she expect to make this season from her orange harvest?

d. Unfortunately, the 16 and a half new rows only produce half of the expected crop yield. What percentage of her expected crop did Rhys actually harvest?

Extend Your Thinking

1. Airspeed is often measured in knots. A knot indicates that a vehicle is moving at 1 nautical mile per hour, which is roughly equivalent to 1.151 miles per hour. Convert the distance between your cities into nautical miles and use the duration of the flight to calculate at how many knots the flight was traveling. Is the ratio of the speed in miles per hour to the speed in knots equivalent to the ratio between miles and nautical miles? Explain why the ratios are equivalent even though one is comparing distance and the other is comparing speed.

NAME:______________________________ DATE:______________

LESSON 3.6

Common Core Assessment Practice

Directions: Complete the problems below.

1. Cole was plotting a graph that showed how the temperature on a mountain changed based on a person's elevation. Which of the following is a true statement?
   - **a.** The temperature is the independent variable and the elevation is the dependent variable.
   - **b.** The elevation is the independent variable and the temperature is the dependent variable.
   - **c.** The mountain is the independent variable and the temperature is dependent.
   - **d.** The temperature is independent and the mountain is the dependent variable.

2. Chandler was riding in a car traveling 60 miles per hour. After 10 minutes, how many feet had Chandler traveled?
   - **a.** 10 feet
   - **b.** 60 feet
   - **c.** 5,280 feet
   - **d.** 52,800 feet

3. The table below represents the amount of money Michael earns based on the number of refrigerators he sells.

Refrigerators	1	2	3	4	5	6
Money	$150	$250	$350	$450	$550	$650

Write an equation to represent this relationship. Let r represent the number of refrigerators and m represent the total money that Michael earns.
   - **a.** $m = 150r$
   - **b.** $m = r + 150$
   - **c.** $m = 100r + 50$
   - **d.** $m = 200r - 50$

Expressions and Equations

4. Colin enjoys mountaineering. As he climbs the mountain, he realizes that for every 500 vertical feet that he climbs the outside temperature drops 2 degrees. At the beginning of his climb, he was at 5,000 feet and the outside temperature was 82 degrees. At the end of his climb, the outside temperature read 68 degrees. How high was Colin when his climb ended?
   a. 3,000 feet
   b. 7,500 feet
   c. 8,500 feet
   d. 9,500 feet

5. Harlan leaves Baton Rouge driving west at a speed of 70 miles per hour. Emma leaves Baton Rouge at the same time driving east at half of Harlan's speed. When Harlan is 350 miles west of Baton Rouge, how far away from Emma is he?
   a. 350 miles
   b. 525 miles
   c. 675 miles
   d. 700 miles

SECTION IV

Geometry

LESSON 4.1

Area of Polygons

Common Core State Standards

- 6.G.A.1
- 6.G.A.3

Mathematical Practices

- 1, 2, 4, 5, and 6

Estimated Time

- 60–90 minutes

Key Terms

- Polygon
- Right triangle
- Vertices
- Quadrilateral

Materials

- Lesson 4.1 Activity: Creating Shapes on a Coordinate Grid
- Lesson 4.1 Coordinate Grid Handout
- Lesson 4.1 Index Cards
- Lesson 4.1 Practice: Geometry on the Coordinate Plane
- Lesson 4.1 Common Core Assessment Practice
- Tape for coordinate grid
- Index cards
- Pieces of string or tape (students should be able to cut off different lengths of pieces)
- Dry-erase boards (optional)
- Sticky notes (optional)

Objectives

In this lesson, students will:

- find the area of polygons,
- compose special polygons made up of different triangles and quadrilaterals, and
- use vertices at different points on a coordinate plane to calculate the area of polygons.

Lesson 4.1 Activity: Creating Shapes on a Coordinate Grid

Use tape to create a coordinate grid on the floor of the classroom. Create a stack of index cards with different points, shapes, and corresponding areas on them. You can use the sample cards provided on Lesson 4.1 Index Cards as examples to make some of your own. Make sure to spread out the locations of the points before the activity starts to ensure that the students are not all clustered in the same location. Students will work in groups of 2–4. The activity will work similar to a relay race. Each group will have its own location on the classroom coordinate grid. Each group will receive the first-level index card that has a vertex (or multiple vertices), a shape, and a required area. The students will be tasked with completing the shape based on the information given to them on the index card. The students should use the coordinate grid to help them find the dimensions they need for each area. For example, a first-level index card might have (2, 3), (2, 4), and (4, 4) as three vertices. The directions would ask the students to plot a fourth point that would create a square with an area of 4 units^2 on the grid. Students will then mark each of the four points on the grid and connect them with a piece of yarn or tape. The four points can be marked by small dry erase boards with the points written on them or something as simple as a sticky note.

Students will write the coordinates for the first level onto Lesson 4.1 Coordinate Grid Handout and show the calculations they completed to find the area. After students have completed the level, they should ask the teacher to check them off and then receive the second-level card. The cards should increase in difficulty as the level get higher. The group that finishes the most levels wins the race.

NAME:______________________________ DATE:______________

LESSON 4.1 ACTIVITY

Creating Shapes on a Coordinate Grid

Directions: Your teacher has transformed your classroom into a coordinate grid! Your group is challenged to complete a series of tasks using your knowledge about the area of polygons and how to find the length of a line using two ordered pairs.

1. One of your group members will receive an index card from your teacher. Your first challenge is written on this card. Plot each of the points on the classroom coordinate grid by marking the point and writing the ordered pair on a dry erase board or sticky note. Plotting the points first will help you visualize the shape that you are trying to create.

2. After you have plotted the points on the index card, plot any additional points needed complete the polygon with the required area.

3. Then, write each of the points down on the Lesson 4.1 Coordinate Grid Handout and show your calculations for the length of each line and the area of the shape formed by each of the points on the grid. Make sure to do the calculations to check your work and make sure your coordinates correctly yield the shape with the required area.

4. When your teacher checks your answer, you will get another index card to complete. Try to complete as many of the index cards as you can before time runs out. Remember to complete the activity sheet with every index card.

Extend Your Thinking

1. Create cards that have the vertices placed in different quadrants on the coordinate grid and use absolute value to find the length of the lines that cross over an axis.

2. Prepare your own cards on which you create a composite shape by combining triangles, rectangles, parallelograms, and trapezoids. You must identify the shape you created as well as calculate the area correctly. List all of the vertices of your composite shape as ordered pairs.

NAME: ______________________________ DATE: ______________

LESSON 4.1
Coordinate Grid Handout

Directions: Write down the vertices for your shape. Calculate the base and height of your shape, and then show your calculations for finding the area of your shape. When you are finished with one shape, get an index card to start working on your next shape. If the shape formed is a trapezoid, indicate both Base 1 and Base 2.

1. Vertices: ____________, ____________, ____________, ____________

Type of shape formed: __________ ; base = __________ , height = __________

Calculate the area of your polygon in the space below:

2. Vertices: ____________, ____________, ____________, ____________

Type of shape formed: __________ ; base = __________ , height = __________

Calculate the area of your polygon in the space below:

3. Vertices: ____________, ____________, ____________, ____________

Type of shape formed: __________ ; base = __________ , height = __________

Calculate the area of your polygon in the space below:

4. Vertices: ____________, ____________, ____________, ____________

Type of shape formed: __________ ; base = __________ , height = __________

Calculate the area of your polygon in the space below:

NAME:__________ DATE:__________

LESSON 4.1

Index Cards

Level 1 Find the area of a rectangle with vertices at (-4, 5), (-4, 7), (2, 5), and (2,7).	**Level 1** Find the area of a triangle with vertices at (7, 2), (4, 2), and (4, -3).
Level 1 Create a rectangle with a base from points (4, 6) and (8, 6) and an area of 4.	**Level 1** Create a triangle with a base from points (1, 1) to (-3, 1) and an area of 8.
Level 2 Create a trapezoid with an area of 6 and one base from (-4,1) to (-1, 1).	**Level 2** Create a parallelogram with an area of 4 and a base from (1, -3) to (5, -3).
Level 2 Create a triangle in Quadrant III with an area of 3.	**Level 2** Create a rectangle in Quadrant II with an area of 6.
Level 2 Create a triangle with an area of 4 that has one vertex at (-4, -4).	**Level 2** Create a triangle with an area of 4.5 that has one vertex at (3, -6).

NAME:______________________________ DATE:______________

LESSON 4.1 PRACTICE

Geometry on the Coordinate Plane

Directions: Complete the problems below.

1. Jordan has created a grid in his back yard in order to plant a garden for the summer. Each one of his paces represents the distance between two points on the grid. He marks the bottom left corner of his garden as the point (-9, -7). He then walks 15 paces up and marks the upper left hand corner of the garden.
   a. At which point did Jordan mark the upper left hand corner?

   b. If Jordan marks the upper right hand corner of the garden at (5, 8) and the bottom right hand corner of the garden at (5, -7), what is the area (in yards) of the entire garden? Assume that one of Jordan's paces measures exactly one yard.

   c. Jordan decides to add a triangular garden space to his garden. His wife wants him to plant peppers for salsa and asks him to create a separate area directly adjacent to the original garden. Jordan begins to section off the triangular garden at point (5, -3). He works down to the bottom right hand corner of the garden (5, -7) and then begins to work to the right. At which point on the garden's grid should Jordan stop sectioning for the triangle to have an area of 8 yards squared?

Geometry

2. Kacie draws a slanted line segment on a sheet of graph paper. The line starts at points (1, 3) and stops at point (4, 6). Using this line, she decides to draw a regular trapezoid that has an area of 18 units squared. She specifically draws the trapezoid in the first quadrant only.
   a. What must the other two vertices of the trapezoid be if the smaller of the two bases on the trapezoid is 3 units?

   b. Think of two other possible pairs of points if no other information is given about the trapezoid other than the area and the two original vertices.

Extend Your Thinking

1. Have you ever noticed the stained-glass windows in old churches? These windows are made up of a number of different pieces of glass. Find a picture of a stained-glass window and section off a rectangular part of the window. Using your best estimate, break up the different pieces of glass into different regular polygons and use them to estimate the area of the glass pieces within the stained-glass window. The purpose of this extension activity is to use your creativity in breaking polygons up into regular polygons. The calculated area should just be a rough estimate instead of an exact number.

NAME:______________________________ DATE:______________

LESSON 4.1

Common Core Assessment Practice

Directions: Complete the problems below.

1. The base of a triangle is formed by the points (-3, 4) and (6, 4). Which of the following points must form the third vertex if the area of the triangle is 27 units squared?
   - **a.** (9, 4)
   - **b.** (-3,10)
   - **c.** (6, -4)
   - **d.** (6, 7)

2. A rectangle is formed by four points: (0, -5), (8, -5), (8, 0), and a fourth point. What is the fourth point?
   - **a.** (0, 0)
   - **b.** (8, 5)
   - **c.** (-5, 8)
   - **d.** (0, 8)

3. A man starts at the point (-3, -7). If the man walks 4 blocks west and 6 blocks south, at what point is the man now standing? Assume each block represents one point on the grid.
   - **a.** (1, -13)
   - **b.** (1, -11)
   - **c.** (-7, -13)
   - **d.** (-9, -11)

4. A man starts at the point (-4, -6) and begins walking east. Every 3 miles that the man walks, he paints a red X on the ground. If he just painted his sixth X, at which point was he standing when he painted it? Assume each mile represents one point on the grid.
   - **a.** (14, -6)
   - **b.** (21, -6)
   - **c.** (18, -6)
   - **d.** (6, -6)

5. What is the difference in area of a rectangle with a base of 4 inches and a height of 6 inches and a triangle with the same base and height?
   - **a.** 0 inches
   - **b.** 6 inches^2
   - **c.** 24 inches^2
   - **d.** 12 inches^2

LESSON 4.2

Volume

Common Core State Standards

- 6.G.A.2

Mathematical Practices

- 1, 2, 3, 4, 5, 6, and 7

Estimated Time

- 60–90 minutes

Key Terms

- Volume
- Rectangular prism
- Pyramid/triangular prism
- Cylinder

Materials

- Lesson 4.2 Activity: Volume in a Vacuum
- Lesson 4.2 Dimension of Spacecraft Throughout History
- Lesson 4.2 Volume of the Ship Worksheet
- Lesson 4.2 Practice: Working With Volume
- Lesson 4.2 Common Core Assessment Practice
- Recyclable materials from which to construct a ship
- Hot glue guns
- Hot glue
- Duct tape
- Rulers

Objectives

In this lesson, students will:

- calculate volume of rectangular prisms, triangular prisms, and cylinders; and
- make decisions based on the volume of an object.

Lesson 4.2 Activity: Volume in a Vacuum

Ever since the first man went into space, people have been brainstorming ways to send humans on longer missions throughout our solar system and beyond. In this activity, students will design a prototype spaceship designed for carrying humans beyond the current scope of space travel. In groups of 3–4, students will brainstorm the necessary components of the ship to accommodate a lengthy space flight. Students should look at examples of ships on Lesson 4.2 Dimension of Spacecraft Throughout History. They can use examples from the International Space Station (information can be found at http://www.nasa.gov) to help them decide what their ship needs. They can also visit http://www.braeunig.us/space/specs.htm to get more information about the different types of space vessels in use. After students have set up the necessary sections, students will use recyclable materials to construct their prototype spaceship.

Students will then use rulers and their understanding of volume formulas to calculate the volume of their spaceship. Teachers can help students scale their volume into real-life dimensions so that students can come up with a plan for what can fit inside their spaceship. Students should brainstorm the different materials that might be needed in each part of the spaceship and decide what can fit and what cannot fit. Each student in the group should take a section of the ship. On Lesson 4.2 Volume of the Ship Worksheet, students should list the materials and goods that should go in that part of the spaceship. While filling out the worksheet, students will estimate the volume of each material in the section of the ship and make sure there is enough room. For example, a person might be thought of as a rectangular prism (for the volume they occupy). Students can then estimate the volume a person might occupy as a rectangular prism. Encourage them to make quick measurements to support their estimations. While the students are doing estimations of volume, they will probably begin to recognize the accuracy and planning that it takes to develop something like the International Space Station.

NAME:______________________________ DATE:______________

LESSON 4.2 ACTIVITY

Volume in a Vacuum

Directions: What would it take for mankind to make a trip past the moon and begin exploring the solar system? What would this space vessel need in order to survive a sustained mission into deep space? For NASA, maximizing the volume of its space vehicles is essential for both cost and travel efficiency. How might you build a ship to complete this mission?

In this activity, you will join a design group of 3–4 students and begin planning a vehicle whose mission is to travel into the deeper parts of our solar system. You must take into account the supplies you might need to bring to complete the mission. There are three types of materials you need to consider: survival materials, science/research materials, and ship operations materials such as fuel, communications, and piloting. How can you and your design team build a ship that can accommodate this mission?

1. Begin by brainstorming the different materials that the voyage would require. Brainstorm as a class and choose the ones that you and your team feel best meets the mission requirements.

2. Estimate the volume needed to hold all of the materials that you plan to bring along. For example, even though it might be difficult to calculate the exact volume taken up by one astronaut, you might estimate that an astronaut is similar enough to a rectangular prism to be able to make a good volume estimate using the formula for the volume of a rectangular prism. Understand, though, that space travel takes extraordinary accuracy and planning, so try to imagine how much work might have to go into finding exact measurements and volumes. On your Lesson 4.2 Volume of the Ship Worksheet, list the items that you need for the journey and explain your justification for each of the items' volume estimations.

3. Bring in recyclable materials such as small cardboard boxes, cans, plastic bottles, and anything else that might be useful in the ship model. On your Lesson 4.2 Volume of the Ship Worksheet, calculate the volume of each of the individual sections that you might use to construct the ship.

4. Using hot glue, duct tape, or another means with which to connect the individual pieces, construct the ship with your design team. Indicate with a marker which section will be used for which function of the trip. One your Lesson 4.2 Volume of the Ship Worksheet, calculate the total volume of the ship.

5. Scale your model's volume to meet human specifications by converting everything into cubic meters.

Extend Your Thinking

1. Volume is at a premium in space shuttles. In fact, careful planning needs to be carried out in order to figure out the most efficient way to transport something to the International Space Station so the astronauts can construct it. If you are planning on sending all of the pieces of your ship to the International Space Station before the spaceship is assembled, you need to research the volume of one of the payload bays of the space shuttles that will carry the pieces of the spaceship up to be assembled at the International Space Station. How could you develop a plan for getting all of the pieces from the ground into space using the payload of one of the space shuttles? Try to keep in mind the cost of sending a shuttle to the International Space Station. You want to get as much as you can into one trip.

2. Research essential items that astronauts on the International Space Station must have in order to successfully accomplish their mission and survive in the harsh conditions of space. Determine what other items are expendable and can be cut in order to make room for the required materials. Discuss the importance of the item related to the volume that it might take up.

NAME:________________________________ DATE:________________

LESSON 4.2

Dimension of Spacecraft Throughout History

Directions: Use this handout to help you brainstorm ideas for creating your own spaceship.

Spacecraft	Habitable Volume	Image
Mercury	1.70 m^3	
Gemini	2.55 m^3	
Apollo	6.17 m^3	
Space Shuttle Orbiter	70.5 m^3	
Orion (Next Gen Space Flight)	10.22 m^3	

Note. Information courtesy of http://braeunig.us/space.

NAME:______________________________ DATE:______________

LESSON 4.2

Volume of the Ship Worksheet

Directions: What sections would you need in order to build a complete spaceship that could travel throughout our solar system? Brainstorm the number of distinct sections you would need to construct as well as the specific function of that section. For example, one section might be used specifically for habitat and living area.

1. First section:
   a. Briefly describe the first section of your ship.

   b. Calculate the scaled volume of this specific section. Show your work below.

   c. Make a list of essential materials you will use in this section and estimate (show your work to defend your estimation) the amount of volume that the materials in this section would occupy.

2. Second section:
   a. Briefly describe the second section of your ship.

b. Calculate the scaled volume of this specific section. Show your work below.

c. Make a list of essential materials you will use in this section and estimate (show your work to defend your estimation) the amount of volume that the materials in this section would occupy.

3. Third section:

a. Briefly describe the third section of your ship.

b. Calculate the scaled volume of this specific section. Show your work below.

c. Make a list of essential materials you will use in this section and estimate (show your work to defend your estimation) the amount of volume that the materials in this section would occupy.

NAME:________________________ DATE:____________

LESSON 4.2 PRACTICE
Working With Volume

Directions: Complete the problems below.

1. A student at an architecture school is designing a model for a replica of a log cabin to be used in a recreation of a scene from American history. The log cabin takes the shape of a rectangular prism. The student's design has a length of 8 inches, a width of 4 inches, and a height of 3 inches.
   a. What is the volume of the model replica log cabin?

   b. If the actual replica is built using a ratio of 5 feet for every 1 inch on the model, what is the volume of the replica?

   c. A company decides to commercialize the log cabin based on the student's design. The company takes the dimensions of the actual replica and multiplies each one by a scale factor of one half. What is the volume of the company's version of the log cabin?

   d. What is the ratio of the volume of the second prism to the volume of the first cube?

e. How is the ratio of volumes related to the scale factor and the formula for finding the volume of a rectangular prism?

2. Caleb works at an aquarium. One of the new designs for a display involves stacking multiple cubic tanks on top of each other with fish inside each of the tanks. Caleb's job is to stack the tanks and fill them up until they are $\frac{4}{5}$ full. Each tank has sides that are 2 feet long.

   a. If there are 12 tanks in all, how many cubic feet will the aquarium's display be in total?

   b. How many cubic feet of water will it take to correctly fill up all 12 tanks?

   c. If Caleb can fill up 0.2 cubic feet of water a minute, how many hours will it take him to get the display ready? Assume that all he has left to do is fill the tanks with water.

Extend Your Thinking

1. Since the first manned spacecraft took off in the 1960s, the capsule has grown from a small, one-manned pod that wasn't even 2 cubic meters in volume to a shuttlecraft more than 70 cubic meters in volume. Look at the different habitable volumes over the course of the years and estimate the dimensional changes of each of the spacecraft. Does the capsule look similar to any of the three-dimensional shapes you have studied in class? Which formula would give you the best estimate for the volume of the capsule? If you aren't familiar with the volume formulas for the shape, you can quickly research it before continuing. Experiment with fractional increases in each of the dimensions to see if you can get close to the increase in volume. What observations can you make about how the changes in dimensions affect the changes in volume?

NAME:____________________ DATE:__________

LESSON 4.2

Common Core Assessment Practice

Directions: Complete the problems below.

1. What is the volume in mm^3 of a rectangular prism whose height is 3 cm, width is 5 cm, and base is 2 cm?
   a. 30 mm^3
   b. 60 m^3
   c. 300 mm^3
   d. 30,000 mm^3

2. What is the ratio of the volume of a cube with a side length of 6 inches and the volume of a cube whose side length is 1 foot?
   a. 1:2
   b. 1:8
   c. 2:1
   d. 1:4

3. What is the volume of a cube whose side length is $\frac{1}{5}$ inch?
   a. 125 $inches^3$
   b. $\frac{1}{25}$ $inches^3$
   c. $\frac{1}{125}$ $inches^3$
   d. 25 $inches^3$

4. A hose has filled $\frac{3}{4}$ of a tank with water. If the tank is a rectangular prism with sides of 4 feet, 5 feet, and 9 feet, how many cubic feet of volume in the tank remains unfilled?
   a. 45 ft^3
   b. 180 ft^3
   c. 60 ft^3
   d. 25 ft^3

5. A room in a European palace is 20 feet by 30 feet by 10 feet. In all four corners of the room there are decorative cubic statues that have a side length of 3 feet. If nothing else is in the room, how much of the volume of the room remains unoccupied?
   a. 4,862 ft^3
   b. 7,986 ft^3
   c. 5,892 ft^3
   d. 492 ft^3

Geometry

LESSON 4.3

Surface Area and Nets

Common Core State Standards

- 6.GA.4

Mathematical Practices

- 1, 2, 3, 4, 6, and 7

Estimated Time

- 60–90 minutes

Key Terms

- Net
- Surface area
- Polyhedron

Materials

- Lesson 4.3 Activity: Nothing but Nets
- Lesson 4.3 Nets Handout
- Lesson 4.3 Polyhedron Handout
- Lesson 4.3 Sample Base Cards and Scaled Factor Slips
- Lesson 4.3 Surface Area Calculation Worksheet
- Lesson 4.3 Practice: Surface Area and Nets
- Lesson 4.3 Common Core Assessment Practice
- Scissors
- Tape
- Example polyhedrons (optional)
- Calculators

Objectives

In this lesson, students will:

- recognize net representations of three-dimensional objects,
- calculate surface area of objects using nets, and
- make predictions based on the changing dimensions of the objects.

Lesson 4.3 Activity: Nothing but Nets

Students will use this activity to explore the relationship between surface area, volume, and a change in dimensions. Students will begin the lesson by matching a net to its corresponding three-dimensional shape. Students should match a net from the Lesson 4.3 Nets Handout to a polyhedron on the Lesson 4.3 Polyhedron Handout. Have the students cut out the nets from their Nets Handout and tape them next to the matching polyhedron on the Polyhedron Handout. You might want to have the polyhedrons taped around the classroom so the students can match them quickly and you can easily reference them in your lesson.

After they have matched the nets and polyhedrons, students will calculate the surface area of a cube and rectangular prism. Students will work in groups of two. To start, students will choose a base card from a stack of index cards (there should be one card for each group). There are sample base cards on the Lesson 4.3 Sample Base Cards and Scaled Factor Slips handout, and you can develop your own. The base card indicates the original dimensions of each polyhedron and functions as the default dimensions for each of the three-dimensional shapes (cube and rectangular prism). Using the nets, students will calculate the surface area for each of the polyhedrons. They should complete their calculations on the Lesson 4.3 Surface Area Calculation Worksheet. As a class, discuss the different surface areas calculated and see if students can generalize a formula for calculating the surface area of the cube and the rectangular prism.

After discussing how to create a formula for calculating the surface area for each of the nets, students will choose a scale-factor slip. There are sample slips on the Lesson 4.3 Sample Base Cards and Scaled Factor Slips handout, and you can develop your own. Students will increase each dimension of their shapes by the scale factor on their card and recalculate the surface area of the object. Students will fill out the Lesson 4.3 Surface Area Calculation Worksheet and then choose a different scale factor slip. Students should complete calculations for each of the new scale factor cards, filling out the Lesson 4.3 Surface Area Calculation Worksheet for each one. After completing the scale factor part of the activity, students should compare the surface areas to the original base surface area.

Encourage students to look for a pattern or relationship between the scale factor increase and the new surface area of the cube and rectangular prism. They should compare the surface area to the base surface area and connect it to the formulas that they used to calculate the surface area of each three-dimensional shape. Ask the students to write a rule for each of the different shapes indicating how an increase (or decrease) in the dimensions of each shape increases or decreases the surface area of that shape. Ask students to make a prediction about the surface area of their shapes if each of the shapes' dimensions were increased by a scale factor of 100. Allow students to use calculators to check their prediction and see if it works with the rule that they wrote.

NAME:______________________________ DATE:______________

LESSON 4.3 ACTIVITY

Nothing but Nets

Directions: What is the relationship between the dimensions of a three-dimensional shape and the surface area of that shape? You are familiar with the formulas for calculating surface area of an object, but can you observe patterns in the change of surface area based on a change in dimensions?

1. First, your teacher will give you a set of nets on the Lesson 4.3 Nets Handout that match a three-dimensional figure. Cut out those nets and tape them next to the corresponding polyhedron found on the Lesson 4.3 Polyhedron Handout.

2. After matching the nets with the three-dimensional shapes, choose a base card from the stack and use the dimensions of each shape to calculate the surface area of each object. Do your calculations on the Lesson 4.3 Surface Area Calculation Worksheet. This base card will be the default dimensions of your polyhedron.

3. With your teacher and classmates, generalize a formula for calculating the surface area of the objects to make the calculations go more quickly. Look for patterns and repetitions in calculations and think about how you could write that as an equation that could be more quickly calculated. Discuss with your group (and class) the characteristics of the shapes for which it is easier to generalize a formula.

4. After you have written down generalizations for your formulas, choose a slip from the scale-factor stack. Increase each of the dimensions in each of your three-dimensional figures by that scale factor and recalculate the surface area. Do your calculations on the Lesson 4.3 Surface Area Calculation Worksheet.

5. Repeat this process for three different scale factor slips. After you have completed your recalculations, compare your surface area to your original calculations. How are the increases related to the scale factor? Generalize a rule for how the increase in dimensions relates to the increase in surface area.

6. Write down a rule and explain how the relationship relates to the formulas for each of the three-dimensional objects.

Extend Your Thinking

1. What would happen if the scale factors were fractions? Think about how an increase by a fractional scale factor would affect the surface area of an object. Make a prediction based on your rule that you generalized in the activity for a rectangular prism. Choose two or three fractional scale factors and change your dimensions based on that scale factor. How did the surface area change based on the scale factor? Did it fit in the rule that you wrote in the original activity?

2. Create scale-factor cards that are fraction scale factors. Generalize a rule for fractional scale factors. Is there a difference between fractional scale factors and whole number scale factors?

NAME:______________________ DATE:______________

LESSON 4.3
Nets Handout

Net 1

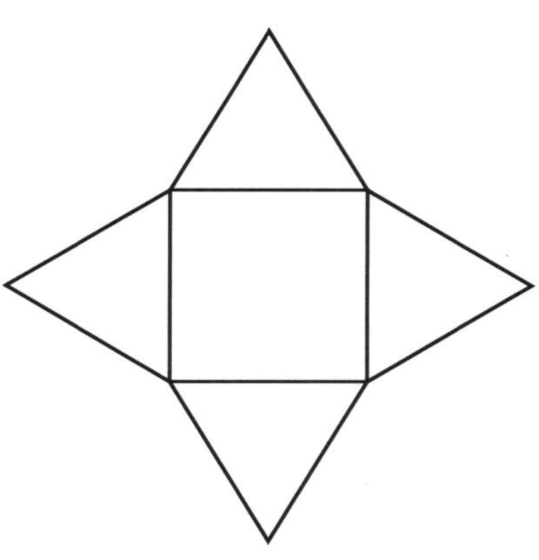

Net 2

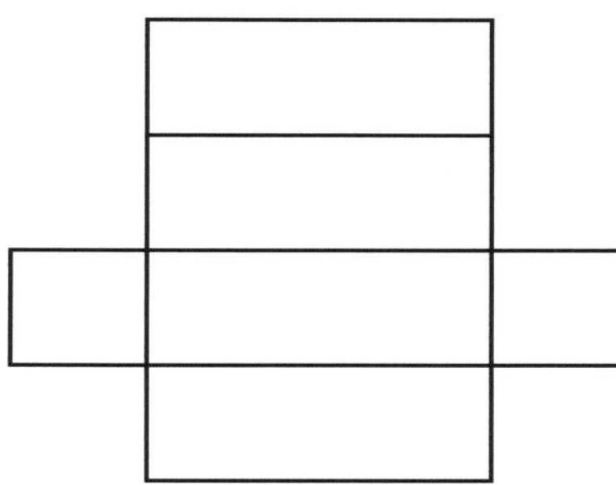

Net 3

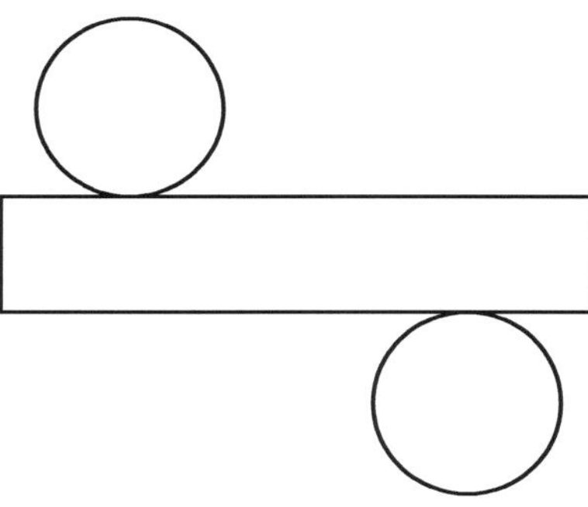

Net 4

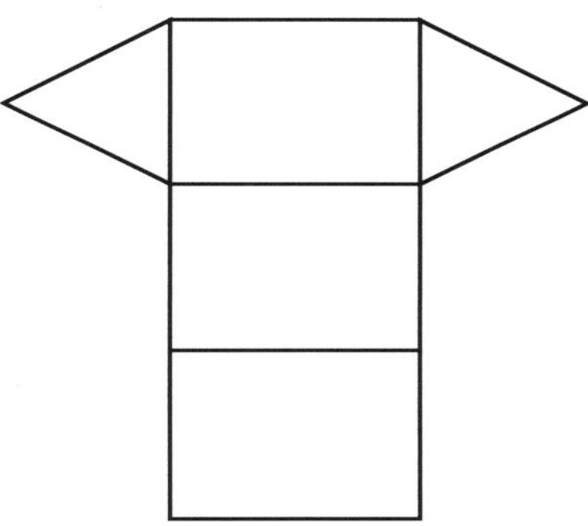

Net 5

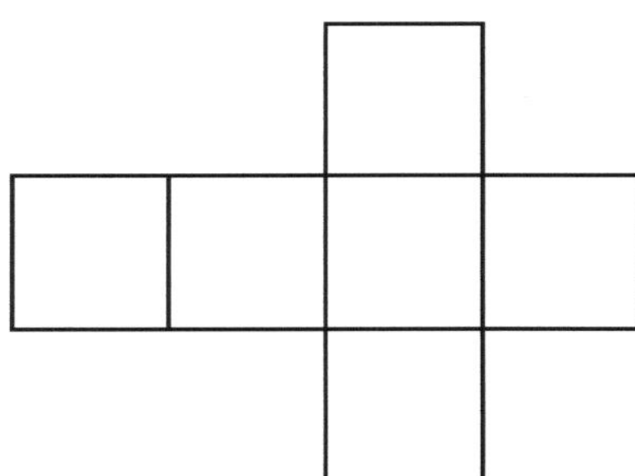

NAME:______________________________ DATE:______________

Geometry

LESSON 4.3
Polyhedron Handout

Polyhedron 1

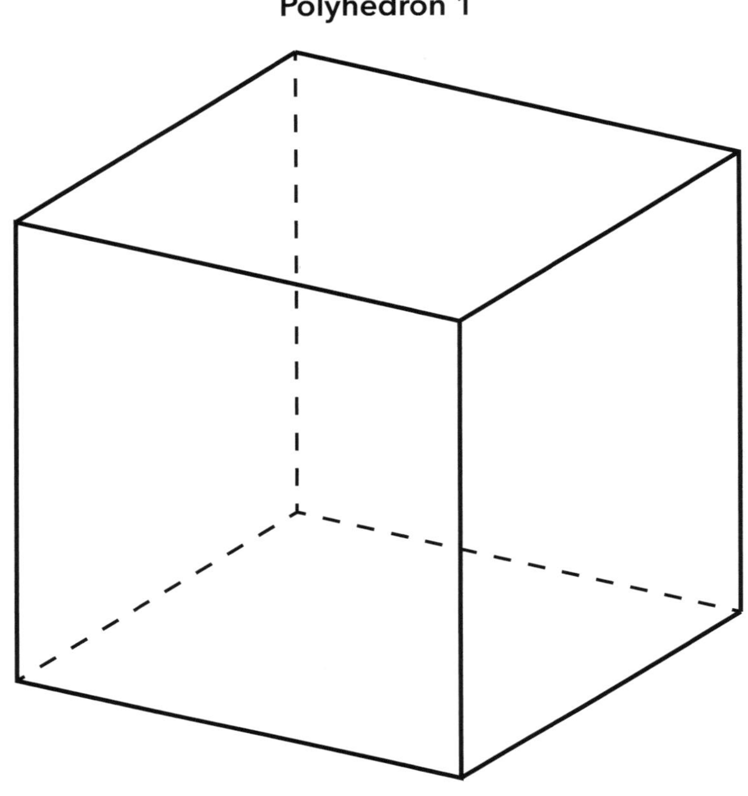

Polyhedron 2

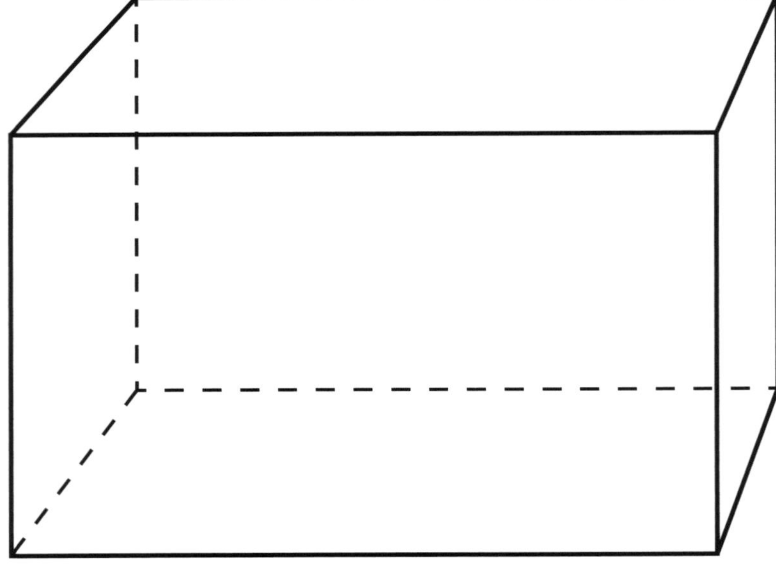

Polyhedron 3

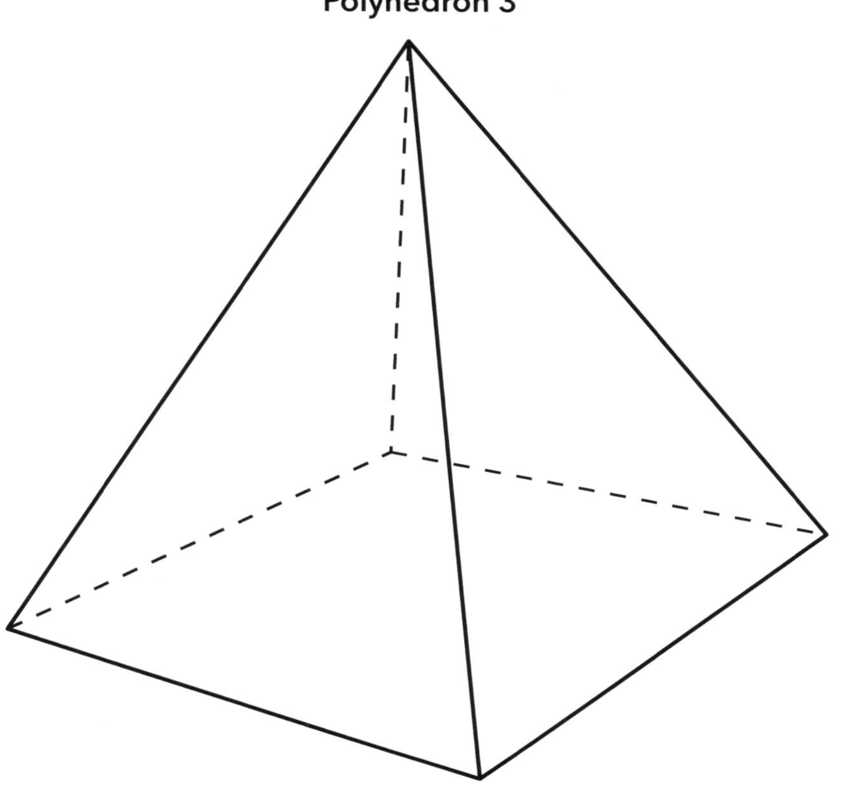

Polyhedron 4

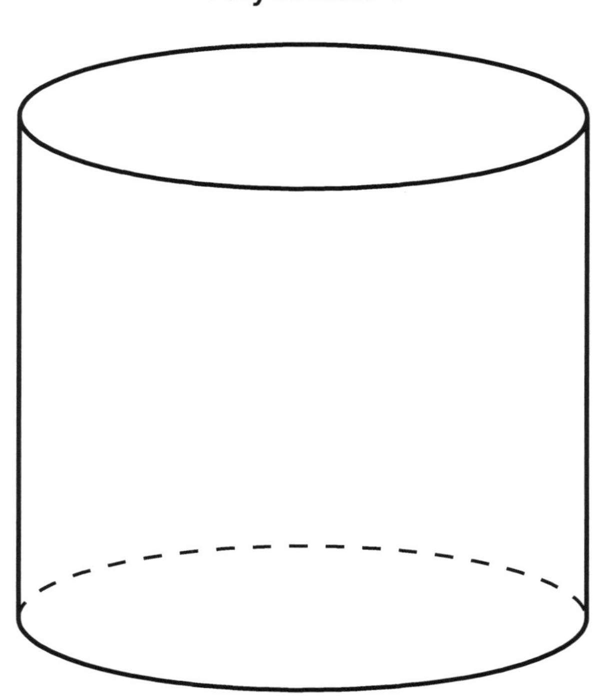

Polyhedron 5

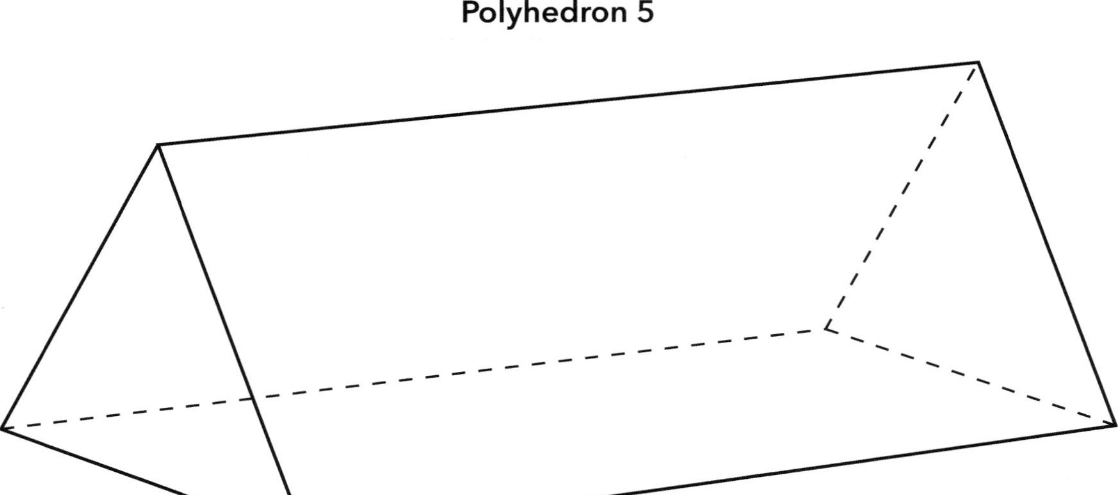

NAME:______________________________ DATE:______________

LESSON 4.3

Sample Base Cards and Scaled Factor Slips

Directions: These are sample base cards that you can use in this activity. Feel free to use these or make your own.

Cube	**Rectangular Prism**	**Cube**	**Rectangular Prism**
Side Length: 4 cm	Length: 2 cm Width: 3 cm Height: 4 cm	Side Length: 5 in	Length: 6 in Width: 2 in Height: 5 in
Cube Side Length: 2 ft	**Rectangular Prism** Length: 8 ft Width: 5 ft Height: 2 ft	**Cube** Side Length: 6 m	**Rectangular Prism** Length: 4 m Width: 1 m Height: 10 m
Cube Side Length: ______	**Rectangular Prism** Length: ______ Width: ______ Height: ______	**Cube** Side Length: ______	**Rectangular Prism** Length: ______ Width: ______ Height: ______
Cube Side Length: ______	**Rectangular Prism** Length: ______ Width: ______ Height: ______	**Cube** Side Length: ______	**Rectangular Prism** Length: ______ Width: ______ Height: ______

These are sample scale factors that you can use in this activity. Feel free to use these or make your own.

Scale Factor (times) 2	**Scale Factor** (times) 3	**Scale Factor** (times) 4	**Scale Factor** (times) 5
Scale Factor (times) 6	**Scale Factor** (times) 7	**Scale Factor** (times) 8	**Scale Factor** (times) 10
Scale Factor (times) $\frac{1}{2}$	**Scale Factor** (times) $\frac{1}{4}$	**Scale Factor** (times) $\frac{1}{5}$	**Scale Factor** (times) $\frac{1}{10}$
Scale Factor (times) ______	**Scale Factor** (times) ______	**Scale Factor** (times) ______	**Scale Factor** (times) ______
Scale Factor (times) ______	**Scale Factor** (times) ______	**Scale Factor** (times) ______	**Scale Factor** (times) ______

NAME:______________________________ DATE:______________

LESSON 4.3

Surface Area Calculation Worksheet

Directions: Calculate the surface area of the cube and rectangular prism. Generalize a formula that would work for calculating the surface area of each object. When you have chosen a scale factor card, calculate the new surface areas. Try to relate that new surface area to the scale factor chosen.

Base Surface Area of Cube:	**Base Surface Area of Rectangular Prism:**
Generalized Formula:	**Generalized Formula:**

1. Scale Factor: ______________________________

New Dimensions of Cube:	New Dimensions of Rectangular Prism:
Surface Area of New Cube:	Surface Area of New Rectangular Prism:

Geometry

2. Scale Factor: ______________________________

New Dimensions of Cube: Surface Area of New Cube:	New Dimensions of Rectangular Prism: Surface Area of New Rectangular Prism:

3. Scale Factor: ______________________________

New Dimensions of Cube: Surface Area of New Cube:	New Dimensions of Rectangular Prism: Surface Area of New Rectangular Prism:

4. Explain how the increases in surface area are related to the scale factor and the formula for calculating the surface area.

5. Generalize a rule for the increase in surface area based on the increase in dimensions (scale factor).

NAME:____________________ DATE:__________

LESSON 4.3 PRACTICE

Surface Area and Nets

Directions: Complete the problems below.

1. Complete the following questions about a cube.
   a. Draw a net to represent a cube that has a side length of 3 cm (not to scale).

   b. On each face of the cube, write the area of that face.
   c. Write a variable expression to represent the surface area of the cube. Calculate the surface area.

2. A rectangular prism has a surface area of 220 meters squared.
   a. If two of the sides have an area of 50 meters squared each, write the possible dimensions of the rectangular prism.

   b. If all of the dimensions of the rectangular prism were multiplied by a scale factor of 2, what will be the new surface area of the rectangular prism?

c. By what scale factor was the surface area increased? How can you relate this scale factor to the scale factor by which the dimensions were increased?

Extend Your Thinking

1. Research the dimensions (including the slant height) of the pyramids at Giza. You can draw a net for each of the pyramids and calculate a surface area for each of the pyramids. After you have drawn a net, calculate a ratio in each of the dimensions and compare it to the surface area of each of the three pyramids. Is the ratio of the dimensions of the pyramid consistent with the differences in the surface area based on observations made in the lesson?

NAME:______________________________ DATE:______________

LESSON 4.3

Common Core Assessment Practice

Directions: Complete the problems below.

1. Which of the following shapes does this net represent?

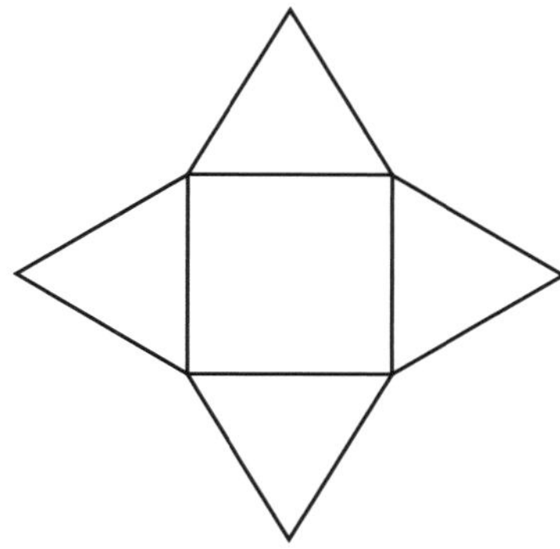

   a. Rectangular prism
   b. Square-based pyramid
   c. Cube
   d. Tetrahedron

2. A triangle with a base of 4 cm and a height of 6 cm is copied and used to make a pyramid with a square base. What is the surface area of the pyramid?
   a. 24 cm^2
   b. 48 cm^2
   c. 64 cm^2
   d. 96 cm^2

3. What is the difference in surface area of a cube with side lengths of 8 inches and a rectangular prism with dimensions of 8 inches, 9 inches, and 10 inches, respectively?
   a. 100 $inches^2$
   b. 250 $inches^2$
   c. 384 $inches^2$
   d. 600 $inches^2$

4. A regular cube with side lengths of 1 inch has a surface area of 6 inches^2. By what scale factor does the surface area change if the cube is shrunk to side lengths of $\frac{1}{4}$ inches?

   a. 16

   b. 4

   c. $\frac{1}{4}$

   d. $\frac{1}{16}$

5. What is the height of the triangle used to form the four sides of a square-based pyramid if the surface area of the pyramid is 40 ft^2 and the area of the pyramid's base is 16 feet^2?
   a. 3 feet
   b. 4 feet
   c. 8 feet
   d. 16 feet

SECTION V

Statistics and Probability

LESSON 5.1

Statistical Analysis

Common Core State Standards

- 6.SP.A.1
- 6.SP.A.2
- 6.SP.A.3

Mathematical Practices

- 1, 2, 3, 4, 5, 6, and 7

Estimated Time

- 60–90 minutes

Key Terms

- Statistical question
- Measure of center
- Measure of variation
- Data set
- Distribution

Materials

- Lesson 5.1 Activity: A Discussion of Data
- Lesson 5.1 Nonstatistical Questions: Examples (cut into strips ahead of time and hand one to each group)
- Lesson 5.1 Data Observations Worksheet
- Lesson 5.1 Practice: Analyzing Data
- Lesson 5.1 Common Core Assessment Practice

Objectives

In this lesson, students will:

- understand statistical variation and how to write a statistical question so that it has variability,
- understand the difference between a measure of center and measure of variation, and
- make observations about a data set and relate the observations to a measure of center and variation.

Lesson 5.1 Activity: A Discussion of Data

Students will begin the lesson by looking at questions that are not statistical questions and have no statistical variability. You can cut and pass out suggestions on the Lesson 5.1 Nonstatistical

Questions: Examples handout or have students come up with their own examples. With a partner, students will discuss how to change their given question so that it becomes a statistical question that will yield a variety of results. For example, asking an individual student how tall he or she is does not yield any statistical variety. Students might realize that asking for the height of each student in the class would offer a wider range of data that can be compared. The question might read: "What is the height in inches of every student in the class?" After the students change their question, split the class into two halves. Students will conduct a survey of one half of the class and then put their data in order from least to greatest. Then, students will make observations about their data by completing the Lesson 5.1 Data Observation Worksheet.

After students have completed the first half of their worksheet, students will then survey the second half of the class and add that data to the data from their original survey. Students will then make observations about their new set of data that includes the original survey data. Students should complete the second half of the Lesson 5.1 Data Observation Worksheet.

When the students have finished completing their Lesson 5.1 Data Observation Worksheets, arrange the students in two circles: a larger circle encircling a smaller circle. Two or three groups should make up the inner circle while the outside circle should be the rest of the class. The teacher should put up the data entries from one of the groups and the students in the inner circle should have a discussion, with the teacher moderating, about observations they can make about the data. The students on the outside part of the circle will be thinking of questions about the data, specifically about the structure of the data and the measures of center and variation. The teacher will then rotate the groups and continue leading the discussion and questions.

At the end of the discussion, students should write a general statement about what they noticed about measures of center, measures of variation, and how outliers affect the data. Students should also write a brief statement about whether or not adding more data entries affects the data observations in any way.

NAME:______________________________ DATE:______________

LESSON 5.1 ACTIVITY

A Discussion of Data

Directions: What is the difference between a question and a statistical question? In this activity, you and your partner are going to find the survey data for a statistical question and make observations about the data's measure of center, measure of variation, and overall structure and distribution.

1. Your teacher will hand out a question that has no statistical variation to each group. Discuss briefly with your partner why it has no statistical variation and then revise the question to make it a statistical question.
   a. Write the question that is not a statistical question below.

   b. Write the question again after you and your partner have changed it to a statistical question.

   c. Why is the second question a statistical question but the first question is not?

2. Your teacher will divide the class into halves. Survey your half of the class using the statistical question that you and your partner developed. Once you have your data, order it from least to greatest.
   a. Make a list of your data values as you interview the first half of your classmates using your statistical question. Write the data below.

b. Order the data from least to greatest.

3. Discuss with your partner observations you can make about your statistical data and write those observation down on the Lesson 5.1 Data Observations Worksheet. Look specifically for where the measure of center might fall as well as the data's measure of variation.

4. Once you have finished this part, you will complete the same survey of the second half of the class. Add these data to your original data sample.
   a. Write the data below.

   b. Combine both sets of data into a larger data set. Write it in numerical order below.

   c. With your partner, make note of how the measure of center or variation may have changed when the new data were added. Complete the second half of the Lesson 5.1 Data Observation Worksheet.

5. Your teacher will divide you into two circles, one outer circle and one inner circle. When you are part of the inner circle, you and the other members of the inner circle will share your observations about the data that the teacher shares from the various groups. It is your job to make observations about the measures of center and variation and agree or disagree with the other members of the circle. When you are part of the outer circle, it is your job to ask questions of the people in the inner circle based on the numbers in the data set. Focus specifically on how the numbers are related to each other and what the numbers mean specifically as it relates to the question that was asked.

6. After the discussion, complete the final part of the Lesson 5.1: Data Observation Worksheet and make general statements about the measure of center and measure of variation based on your set of data. Explain how adding more data entries affected the structure of the data.

Extend Your Thinking

1. Calculate the mean of the data that you collected. Compare the mean of the data to your observations that you made about the measure of center. Is the mean different from your measure of center? Why might that be? Explain your answer.

2. You and your partner have made observations about the measure of variation. Why does your data have a specific measure of variation? Think about reasons why the range might be limited to certain numbers. For example, if you collect survey data on siblings for your classmates, why might the range of data be limited to a certain number of siblings?

NAME:__________ DATE:__________

LESSON 5.1
Nonstatistical Questions: Examples

How many letters are in my name?
How many pieces are in this bag of candy?
How tall am I?
How many hours of TV do you watch in one day?
How many hours a night do you spend working on homework?
How many times a week do I eat out at a restaurant?
How many followers do I have on Instagram (or a different social media)?
How many people are you following on Twitter (or a different social media)?
About how many text messages do I send in a day?
How many books do you read in a semester?
How many states have I visited?
How many different pairs of shoes do you own?
How many state capitals can you name off the top of your head?
What is your grade point average?
How long does it take me to get to school in the morning?
In how many extracurricular activities do I participate?
How many stuffed animals/action figures do you own?
How many siblings do I have?
How many weddings have you attended?
Approximately how many items of "junk food" are currently in your house?
How many bones have you broken?

NAME:______________________ DATE:______________

LESSON 5.1
Data Observations Worksheet

Part I: After interviewing the first half of the class, answer the following questions.

1. What observations can you make about the measure of center? Is there a number or range of numbers around which most of the data falls?

2. Based on your statistical question, why do you think the data fall mostly around a specific number or range of numbers?

3. What is the measure of variation? Why do you think all of the numbers fall in this range?

Part II: After interviewing the second half of the class, answer the following questions.

1. Did your measure of center change or did the numbers continue to fall near a number or range of numbers?

2. If the measure of center shifted a bit, what does that tell you about your original set of data? If the measure of center stayed relatively the same, what statement can you make about your data?

3. How does the number of data items in your data set determine the accuracy of your data?

Part III: Based on what you've learned, think about generalizations.

1. How can you look at a set of data and make predictions about its measure of center?

2. How might the type of statistical question you ask affect the variation of your data? Give examples from your classmates to support your answer.

3. How might outliers affect a person's interpretation and understanding of a set of data?

4. Based on your answer to Question 3, should outliers just be ignored? Why or why not?

NAME:______________________________ DATE:______________

LESSON 5.1 PRACTICE

Analyzing Data

Directions: Complete the problems below.

1. Jackson scored a 75, 86, 92, and 88 on his first four tests in his science class.
   a. What is his current average in the class?

   b. What score would Jackson need to make on his fifth test to push his average to an 87%?

   c. Jackson scores a 90 on his fifth test. The teacher decides to drop the lowest score that he made during the year. What is his final average of the four tests the teacher counted?

2. Look at the following question: How many states has Bethenney visited?
   a. Is this an example of a statistical question? Explain why or why not.

   b. How could you rewrite the question so that it yields statistical variation?

c. Based on your question from Part A, what might you expect the data responses to be from the students in your class? List five.

d. Interview five students in your class and ask them your statistical question. Compare their answers to your predicted data. If they are the same, explain why. If they are different explain why that might be the case.

Extend Your Thinking

1. Learn about the process of political polling and how it is used to make predictions in elections and drive the course of public policy. Using a statistical question, survey as many students outside of class as you can. As you survey the students, make observations about whether the data becomes more centered on their observed measure of center or whether the data moves away from the measure of center.

2. Based on your observations, write a brief paragraph explaining the importance of sample size and whether your original data was an accurate representation or not. Write an opinion about the accuracy of polling data and whether it is a viable way to determine the views of the American public.

NAME:______________________________ DATE:______________

LESSON 5.1

Common Core Assessment Practice

Directions: Complete the problems below.

1. Which of the following questions is a statistical question?
   a. How many brothers and sisters does Claire have?
   b. Which flavors of ice cream are Brianna's favorite?
   c. How many students are in each class at Polk High School?
   d. How long was the last movie that Jim watched?

2. Explain how the measure of center would be affected by adding a value of 15 to a data set with a mean of 5.
   a. There would be no effect.
   b. The measure of center would increase, but there is not enough information to determine by how much.
   c. The measure of center would decrease, but there is not enough information to determine by how much.
   d. There is not enough information to answer this question.

3. Explain how the measure of variation of a set of data would be affected by adding the value of 75 to a data set with a range of 12.
   a. There would be no effect.
   b. The measure of center would increase, but there is not enough information to determine by how much.
   c. The measure of center would decrease, but there is not enough information to determine by how much.
   d. There is not enough information to answer this question.

4. Which of the following measures of center would be least likely to be affected by adding a number to a data set?
   a. Range
   b. Mean
   c. Mode
   d. Median

5. If you have a data set with a range of 12 and a mean of 65, which of the following numbers would be least likely to be included in the data set?
   a. 60
   b. 85
   c. 67
   d. 65

LESSON 5.2

Representing Data in Graphs

Common Core State Standards

- 6.SP.B.4
- 6.SP.B.5

Mathematical Practices

- 1, 2, 3, 4, 5, 6, 7, and 8

Estimated Time

- 60–90 minutes

Key Terms

- Mean
- Median
- Mode
- Range
- Dot plot
- Histogram
- Box plot

Materials

- Lesson 5.2 Activity: Defending a Data Set
- Lesson 5.2 Data Sets
- Lesson 5.2 Graphing Data
- Lesson 5.2 Defending a Data Set Worksheet
- Lesson 5.2 Practice: Analyzing Sets of Data
- Lesson 5.2 Common Core Assessment Practice

Objectives

In this lesson, students will:

- calculate the measures of center and variation for a set of data;
- plot the data in a dot plot, histogram, and box plot; and
- evaluate the measures of center based on observations of a set of data.

Lesson 5.2 Activity: Defending a Data Set

Students will begin the lesson by looking at the provided list of three data sets on the Lesson 5.2 Data Sets handout. Students will calculate the mean, median, mode, and range for all three of the data lists. After the students have calculated the measures of center and measure of variation, the students will plot the points on the three graphs on the Lesson 5.2 Graphing Data worksheet. As a class, discuss the measure of center that would best represent each of the three data sets. Students will then write a paragraph describing the best and worst measure of center for each data set and use their graphs to defend their answer. Students should write their paragraph on the Lesson 5.2 Defending a Data Set Worksheet. Encourage students to use examples from each of their three graphs to defend their answers.

As students finish their paragraphs, have a few of them share their ideas and hold a brief discussion on correct and incorrect observations. Ask students to make a generalization for types of data sets where each measure of center might be best. Students should write the generalization on the Lesson 5.2 Defending a Data Set Worksheet.

After the discussion and the generalization of rules, students will choose an outlier for one of the three data sets and incorporate that outlier into the data set. Students will then recalculate the measures of center for that data set and determine how much the outlier affects each of the measures of center. Students will write a generalization about which measure of center to use with outliers on the Lesson 5.2 Defending a Data Set Worksheet.

NAME:______________________________ DATE:______________

LESSON 5.2 ACTIVITY
Defending a Data Set

Directions: As you have probably figured out by now, data are not just a set of random numbers with no relationship between them. But just how far does the relationship go? In this activity, you will dig a little deeper into the measures of center and variation to analyze the relationships between the numbers and how adding or taking out certain numbers will affect the data set as a whole.

1. First, look over the three data sets that your teacher has provided and hypothesize which graph would be best for which set of data. Then, take the three data sets that your teacher has provided you on Lesson 5.2 Data Sets and plot them on the three graphs on the Lesson 5.2 Graphing Data worksheet. Use one set of data for each of the three graphs provided to you. Look at each graph and draw conclusions about the positives (and negatives) for using a certain type of graph with a data set. Your conclusions may differ from your original hypothesis. Which graph do you feel best represents the data that you plotted?

2. Calculate the mean, median, mode, and range for each of the different data sets.

	Data Set 1	Data Set 2	Data Set 3
Mean			
Median			
Mode			
Range			

3. On your Lesson 5.2 Defending a Data Set Worksheet, analyze the three graphs and the measures of center for each graph. Write down which measure of center best represents each data set. What characteristics do you notice about the data that might make a measure of center more or less useful?

4. Write a paragraph that explains your observations and defends your observations with examples from your graphs.

5. Discuss with your class observations about the data that make them stronger or weaker.

6. Look at the outlier for each set of data. Put the outlier into each data set and recalculate the measures of center.

7. Explain on Lesson 5.2 Defending a Data Set Worksheet which measures of center are most and least affected by an outlier. Explain why you think that might be. Hint: Think about which numbers in the data set are used to calculate each measure of center.

Extend Your Thinking

1. Now that you have calculated the mean of your data set, pull out the lowest and highest data value in your set. Make a prediction of how the mean will be affected by the change. Do you think it will increase or decrease? After you calculate the mean, compare it to the prediction and explain why you were right or wrong. Which number is having a larger effect on the mean? Why might that be? For example, you might notice that the mean went up a little after both numbers were taken out of the set. You might notice that the lower number was further away from the mean than the higher number, which might explain the rise.

NAME:____________________ DATE:__________

LESSON 5.2

Data Sets

Data Set 1

Test Scores in High School Biology:

89, 87, 85, 84, 90, 79, 83, 85, 86, 88, 84, 81, 88, 85, 83, 83, 86, 82, 83, 86, 84

Outlier: 45

Data Set 2

Number of Miles Driven by Trucks at a Shipping Company in a Day:

123, 313, 531, 533, 80, 535, 542, 543, 223, 549, 890, 754, 552, 553, 554, 128, 560, 561, 563, 563, 563, 900

Outlier: 0

Data Set 3

Number of Siblings for Students in a Class:

1, 0, 2, 2, 2, 4, 2, 2, 1, 5, 2, 2, 2, 6, 0, 0, 2, 2, 3, 3, 2, 2, 3, 4

Outlier: 12

NAME:____ DATE:____________________

LESSON 5.2

Graphing Data

Directions: Choose the graph that would best accommodate the set of data. Graph the three data sets into a dot plot, box plot, and histogram. As you are graphing the points, you may notice patterns that work better for a specific graph that is different than you expected. For example, you may believe that a box plot is best for a specific set of data but when you start graphing it, you realize that a histogram might be better. Graph the same data set as a histogram and draw conclusions that support your reason for the change.

1. Dot Plot — Data Set: ____________________

   Why does the dot plot best fit this set of data?

2. Histogram — Data Set: ____________________

   Why does the histogram best fit this set of data?

Statistics and Probability

3. Box Plot

Data Set: ______________________

Why does the box plot best fit this set of data?

NAME:______________________ DATE:__________

LESSON 5.2

Defending a Data Set Worksheet

1. For which data set would the mean be the best measure of center?

2. For which data set would the median be the best measure of center?

3. For which data set would the mode be the best measure of center?

4. Write a paragraph explaining your answer for Question 1. Use examples from the data set and graph to support your answer.

5. Write a paragraph explaining your answer for Question 2. Use examples from the data set and graph to support your answer.

6. Write a paragraph explaining your answer for Question 3. Use examples from the data set and graph to support your answer.

7. After discussing and sharing your paragraphs with your class/group members, generalize the type of data set where it would be most appropriate to use each measure of center.
   a. For which types of data would it be best to use the mean as the measure of center? Why?

   b. For which types of data would it be best to use the median as the measure of center? Why?

   c. For which types of data would it be best to use the mode as the measure of center? Why?

8. After using the outliers in your data sets, explain how each measure of center (mean, median, and mode) is affected by the outlier. Defend your answer.

NAME:________________________________ DATE:________________

LESSON 5.2 PRACTICE

Analyzing Sets of Data

Directions: Complete the problems below.

1. Use the following test scores from Mrs. Carmichael's fourth-grade social studies class:

   56, 78, 98, 74, 88, 97, 85, 90, 79, 92

   a. Draw a histogram below to represent the data.

   b. Calculate the mean, median, mode, and range of the data.

   c. Which of the values above could be an outlier? How might the teacher explain that test score?

d. Mrs. Carmichael decides to exclude the largest and smallest values from her calculations to see if her students understood most of the material. What is the mean of the test scores after dropping the top and bottom scores?

e. Why did the mean rise so much even though both the top and bottom scores were dropped?

Extend Your Thinking

1. Choose an NBA player and track his points scored over the course of 10 games. Find the average points scored by your player during that 10 game sample. Then, look back at the last 10 days and find the high temperature for each of those days. Calculate the mean temperature for those 10 days. Use both means to make a prediction for the high temperature and points scored by the NBA player over the next 5 days (or 5 games). Which one of your predictions was more accurate? Explain why you think that this is.

NAME:______________________________ DATE:______________

LESSON 5.2

Common Core Assessment Practice

Directions: Complete the problems below.

1. Which of the following measures would not be 7 in the following data set?

   7, 7, 7, 7, 7, 7, 7

   a. Range
   b. Mode
   c. Median
   d. Mean

2. If Judy has scored an 85, 95, 88, and 92 on her four tests, what does her fifth test need to be to bring her overall average up to a 91?
   a. 91
   b. 94
   c. 95
   d. 100

3. A bus carried 50 children on Monday, 45 children on Tuesday, 52 children on Wednesday, and 58 children on Thursday. If the bus averaged 52 children over the 5-day work week, how many children did the bus carry Friday?
   a. 52
   b. 53
   c. 55
   d. 57

4. Looking at the following box plot, what is the maximum number of music sales in a week?

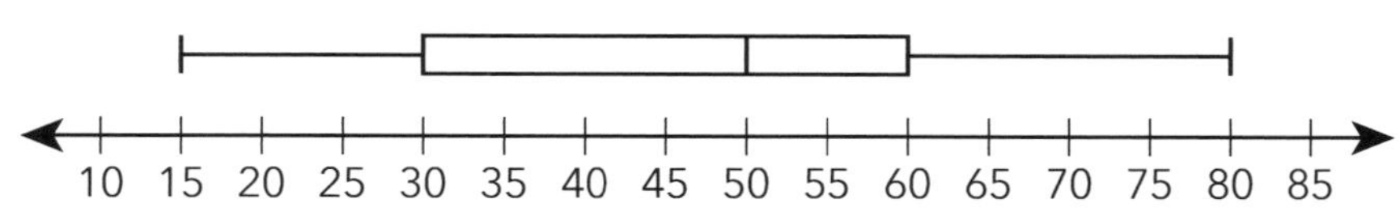

   a. 50
   b. 55
   c. 75
   d. 80

5. If there are 6 items in a data set and the median is 24, which of the following pairs of numbers could not be the 3rd and 4th item in the data set (listed in numerical order)?
   a. 20, 30
   b. 22, 26
   c. 23, 25
   d. 15, 33

ANSWER KEY

SECTION I: RATIOS AND PROPORTIONAL RELATIONSHIPS

Lesson 1.1 Activity: A Bazaar Relationship of Ratios

Answers will vary.

Extend Your Thinking

1. Answers will vary.
2. Answers will vary.
3. Answers will vary.

Lesson 1.1 Bazaar Ratio Table for Exchange Rates

Answers will vary.

Lesson 1.1 Bazaar End-of-Day Graphing Worksheet

Answers will vary.

Lesson 1.1 Practice: Using Ratios

1. a. No

   b.

Classroom(s)	1	2	3	4
Teachers	1	2	3	4
Students	9	18	27	36

   c. Answers will vary.

   d. 135 total students

2. a. 150 women and 400 total passengers; b. 250 men; c. 3:5; d. 390 men to 210 women, for a ratio of 13:7
3. a. 75 beads; b. 10 ribbons for every 6 bracelets or 5 ribbons for every 3 bracelets; c. 50 ribbons, 30 bracelets

Extend Your Thinking

1. Answers will vary.
2. Answers will vary.

Lesson 1.1 Common Core Assessment Practice

1. d
2. a
3. c
4. a
5. d

Lesson 1.2 Activity: Rate Your Products

Answers will vary.

Extend Your Thinking

1. Answers will vary. This could potentially have a wide range of answers, but students might notice that the off-brand items are generally the better buys. They also might notice that items that are larger sized will be better buys that the smaller sized items (in terms of ounces). As the teacher shows similar products, students (when making guesses) can support their guesses with these examples above.
2. Answers will vary. The items, ultimately, are not as important as the final unit price. If students use the example in the problem it might look something like this:

Item	Guacamole 4 ounces	Black Beans 3 ounces	Corn 2 ounces	Sour Cream 1 ounce
Unit Price	\$0.58	\$0.09	\$0.06	\$0.18
Price in Recipe	(0.58×4) \$2.32	(0.09×3) \$0.27	(0.06×2) \$0.12	(0.18×1) \$0.18

The unit price for the four-layer dip would be \$2.89.

3. Answers will vary. If you use three boxes of cereal a month, and the better buy in cereal saves you \$0.49 a box, you would save \$1.47 a month by purchasing the better buy. This should be similar for all products used. Students may notice that purchasing the better buy for one item won't save them much, but if they do it for all of the items on their grocery list it may turn into more significant savings.

Lesson 1.2 Unit Price Comparison

1. Answers will vary. For example, Zevia Caffeine-Free Cola has a price of \$22.40. The product is measured in fluid ounces. The product contains a total of 288 fluid ounces, so the unit price is \$0.08 per ounce.
2. Answers will vary. For example, Hansen's Diet Black Cherry Cola has a price of \$16.89. The product is measured in fluid ounces. The product contains a total of 288 fluid ounces, so the unit price is \$0.06 per ounce.
3. Answers will vary. For example, Vernor's Ginger Ale has a price of \$14.33. The product is measured in fluid ounces. There are 288 fluid ounces, so the unit price is \$0.05 per ounce.
4. Answers will vary. Students should divide the cost of the items by the total number of fluid ounces (or other measurement) in their product.

5. Answers will vary. Students may realize that because all of the ounces are the same (as shown in the examples) that they can just compare price per 288 ounces instead of calculating the unit price for each. Students may also realize that they can just convert each price to a common amount to make an easier comparison.

Lesson 1.2 Advertisement Storyboard

Answers will vary.

Lesson 1.2 Practice: Comparing Unit Price

1. a. $12.55; b. $360.00; c. $9,412.50 in total sales; $5,400.00 in profit
2. a. $4.15; b. 1,302 shirts; c. 362 shirts

Extend Your Thinking

1. Answers will vary.

Lesson 1.2 Common Core Assessment Practice

1. b
2. d
3. c
4. b
5. a

Lesson 1.3 Activity: A Healthier Percent

Answers will vary.

Extend Your Thinking

1. Answers will vary. If a student eats a total of 2,000 calories in a day and categorizes 1,200 calories as "bad" foods and 800 calories as "good" foods, he would have 60% of his food as unhealthy and 40% of his food as healthy.
2. Answers will vary.
3. Answers will vary. Students may realize that 1,200 calories of their diet are coming from grains when all they need is 500. They will calculate that they need to decrease these calories by about 58%.

Lesson 1.3 Practice: Calculate the Percent

1. a. 15%; b. 625 calories; c. 29%
2. a. 26%; b. 14.4 acres for green beans, 30 acres for corn, 15.6 acres for tomatoes; c. 22.5 acres; d. The total earnings of green beans is $72,000; the total earnings of corn is $225,000 and the total earnings of tomatoes is $124,800. 29.5% or 30%.

Extend Your Thinking

1. Answers will vary.

Lesson 1.3 Common Core Assessment Practice

1. c
2. b
3. c
4. a
5. d

Lesson 1.4 Activity: Converting Units Taboo

Answers will vary.

Extend Your Thinking

1. Answers will vary.

Lesson 1.4 Practice: Converting Units

1. a. 40 times; b. 400 minutes; c. 240 fish
2. a. 39 days; b. $105,600; c. 2.86 miles per hour

Extend Your Thinking

1. Answers will vary.

Lesson 1.4 Common Core Assessment Practice

1. b
2. a
3. d
4. c
5. b

SECTION II: THE NUMBER SYSTEM

Lesson 2.1 Activity: Fractions of a Class Change

Answers will vary based on individual numbers.

Extend Your Thinking

1. Answers will be based on the calculations done in the activity. The petition will vary from student to student.
2. Answers will vary. Students will probably notice the difference in distances with a faster pace. Students should focus on just how much the difference is compared to their normal walk.

Lesson 2.1 Practice: Applications Using Fractions and Decimals

1. a. 64 fence posts; b. 39.5 inches, 3.3 feet; c. Area = 16,900 square feet for the area (130 feet x 130 feet), Perimeter = 520 feet (130 feet x 4)

2. a. \$34.20. Because the deliveryman earns \$0.75 for every mile that he drives, you would multiply $45\frac{3}{5}$ by \$0.75 to figure out the money earned so far that day. Students will probably want to convert $45\frac{3}{5}$ to a decimal (45.60) to solve the problem; b. $154\frac{2}{5}$ or 154.4 miles; c. \$405 or $150 \times .18 = 27 \times 5 = 135 \times 3 = 405$; d. 28% or $(150 \times N) \times 5 = 210$

Extend Your Thinking

1. Answers will vary.
2. Answers will vary.

Lesson 2.1 Common Core Assessment Practice

1. c
2. b
3. a
4. a
5. b

Lesson 2.2 Activity: Creating Monster Multiples

Answers will vary.

Extend Your Thinking

1. Answers will vary.
2. Answers will vary.

Lesson 2.2 Practice: Factors and Multiples

1. a. 3, 5, 15; b. 15 bags; c. 3 muffins and 4 rolls in each bag
2. a. 12 minutes; b. 5 times; c. Judith has run 15 laps, and Augustina has run 10 laps.

Extend Your Thinking

1. Answers will vary.

Lesson 2.2 Common Core Assessment Practice

1. c
2. d
3. b
4. d
5. a

Lesson 2.3 Activity: Positive and Negative Narrative

1. One underline = positive; two underlines = negative
   The sun splintered down on the tundra below
   A warmth filled the air and the temperature rose
   It climbed and it climbed some 15 degrees
   There was hardly a sign of the danger, the freeze.

Bartholomew worked in his Antarctic lab
Testing the ice, slab after slab
Bristled and burned, his fingers afire
He was beginning to slow; he was beginning to tire
Careless, an ice block fell to the floor
It shattered and fractured into pieces galore
Out of the core of ice rose a harsh scream
And the pieces that scattered all melted to steam
The lights in the lab went instantly black
The temperature plunged 40 degrees with a crack
Bartholomew, frightened, threw on his jacket
And ran out the door to escape all the racket
By the time he looked up the sun was scarce to be found
His feet slipped and he slid over the ice-covered ground
Shaking all over, he looked with a shock
The temperature outside had dropped like a rock
Well below zero, it continued to fall
It fell 30 degrees before beginning to stall
Worn down and wearied he ran from the air
He started a fire with one of his flares
With the flame from the flare he warmed up his toes
He heated his hands and thawed out his nose
The air warmed around him from the heat and the glow
Twenty-five degrees warmer though still very low
Bartholomew saw and realized with fear
The flare's light was waning and the warmth's end was near.
Before the light faded he looked at his gauge
"Seventy-five below zero," he read with great rage
The dark closed around him and he let out a scream
He woke with a start and realized it was all just a dream
Bartholomew read the thermometer clear
It read 75 degrees, and he shouted a cheer.

2. See answers for Lesson 2.3 Narrative Poem Worksheet.

Extend Your Thinking

1. Answers will vary based on the narrative poem or short story written.
2. Answers will vary based on the narrative poem or short story written. Students should realize that subtracting two negative numbers is similar to adding the two negatives together. Adding a positive number with a negative number is similar to subtracting the two numbers. Students may also notice that adding a negative number is like subtracting, and subtracting a negative number is similar to adding. Students should notice that if one subtracts a number that is larger than the original number, the difference will be negative.

Lesson 2.3 Narrative Poem Worksheet

1. a. rose, climbed, plunged, dropped, fell, warmed; b. Answers will vary.
2. 15, -40, -30, 25, -75, 75
3. -75 and 75 are both opposites because they have equal absolute values (distance from zero).
4. Answers will vary.
5. Answers will vary.
6. Answers will vary.
7. Answers will vary.

Lesson 2.3 Practice: Using Positive and Negative Numbers

1. a. ascent: 1,500, descent: -2,700; b. loss of 1,200 or -1,200; c. 1,050 feet per day; d. 0 feet; e. -6,000
2. a. 1,500; b. $750, -750; c. -500

Extend Your Thinking

1. Answers will vary.

Lesson 2.3 Common Core Assessment Practice

1. d
2. a
3. a
4. b
5. b

Lesson 2.4 Activity: Mapping a Novel

Answers will vary.

Extend Your Thinking

1. Answers will vary.
2. Answers will vary.

Lesson 2.4 Coordinate Grid Setting Map

Answers will vary.

Lesson 2.4 Setting Map

Answers will vary.

Lesson 2.4 Practice: Coordinate Grids

1. a. (-3, 0); b. Answers will vary. Students should indicate and reference cardinal directions. They should make the assertion that because going west is similar to going "left" on a map, students will go left from the origin three units to (-3, 0); c. Answers will vary. Because each line on the grid represents a block, students might place an ordered pair at intervals of 0.5 increasing the y-value. Some sample points might be (-3, 0.5); (-3, 1); (-3, 1.5); and so on; d. 5 blocks south and 2 blocks west; e. 5 miles
2. a. 6 miles; b. 3 miles; c. 10 miles; d. 33 miles

Extend Your Thinking

1. Answers will vary.

Lesson 2.4 Common Core Assessment Practice

1. d
2. a
3. b
4. d
5. a

Lesson 2.5 Activity: Absolute Value of a Skyline

Answers will vary.

Extend Your Thinking

1. Answers will vary.
2. Answers will vary.

Lesson 2.5 Absolute Value Skyline Worksheet

Answers will vary.

Lesson 2.5 Practice: Applications of Absolute Value

1. a. |8.4|; b. |-7.5|; c. 43.6 inches
2. a. |-2,146|, |0|, |735|; b. 25,146 feet; c. |1,045|; d. Group 1: 25,450, Group 2: 26,445, Group 3: 24,246

Extend Your Thinking

1. Answers will vary.

Lesson 2.5 Common Core Assessment Practice

1. b
2. d
3. c
4. c
5. d

SECTION III: EXPRESSIONS AND EQUATIONS

Lesson 3.1 Activity: Power of a Collage

Answers will vary.

Extend Your Thinking

1. Answers will vary.
2. Answers will vary.

Lesson 3.1 Practice: Exponential Expressions

1. a. 3^1; b. 9 children; c. 3×3, 3^2; d. 729. Going by the pattern, each generation can be represented by a base of 3 raised to the power of that generation. There are 243 children in the 5th generation (3^5), and if each one of them has three children, the fifth generation will have 729 children total.
2. a. 16 people. The fourth round involves 8 parents making calls; because each parent calls 2 parents, there are 16 people called during the fourth round; b. 125 people. The third round at Lowland Elementary involves 25 parents making calls; because each parent calls 5 parents, there are 125 parents called in all during the third round; c. 255 parents; d. 50 minutes. For Lowland Elementary, each round of calls takes 30 minutes. Because there are four rounds of calls (4×30 minutes), the total duration of the phone tree is 120 minutes. Highland Elementary takes 10 minutes to complete each round of calls. There are seven rounds for Highland Elementary (7×10 minutes), so it will take 70 minutes to complete the phone tree. To find the difference, subtract 70 from 120 minutes.

Extend Your Thinking

1. Answers will vary.

Lesson 3.1 Common Core Assessment Practice

1. c
2. a
3. c
4. d
5. b

Lesson 3.2 Activity: Chess and Expressions

Answers will vary. Example answers are included below:

A3: $3(5+y)+8x+12-2x+9y$ (Distributive Property)
A4: $12y+4+21x$ (Combining Terms)
A5: $5(50+6)+8\times 85+13+26$ (Distributive Property)
A6: $9\times 24+4\times 36+300-25$ (Distributive Property)
B3: $(15+45)+(23+37)+(12+38)$ (Commutative and Associative Properties of Addition)
B4: $(19+11)+(32+28)+(37+13)$ (Commutative and Associative Properties of Addition)
B5: $40+12y+12x$ (Combining Terms)
B6: $(28+152)+(49+21)+(17+83)$ (Commutative and Associative Properties of Addition)
C3: $6(100+50+2)+8\times 23+9(140-1)$ (Distributive Property)
C4: $2(150-1)+3(100+40)+8\times 29$ (Distributive Property)
C5: $4\times 20+5\times 30+9\times 80$ (Distributive Property)
C6: $5(4y+6)+5(4x)$ (Commutative Property of Addition and Distributive Property)
D3: $15(5+32+42)$ (Distributive Property)

D4: $(12+92+36)+(33+77)$ (Commutative and Associative Properties of Addition)

D5: $3(3y+4y+5y)+4(x+2x+4x)$ (Commutative Property of Addition and Distributive Property)

D6: $30(18+7+1)$ (Distributive Property)

E3: $(12+58)+(17+93)+(19+31)$ (Commutative and Associative Properties of Addition)

E4: $6(50+6)+8\times 48+9\times 71$ (Distributive Property)

E5: $17(1+2)+19(1+2)+15(1+2)$ (Commutative Property of Addition and Distributive Property)

E6: $4(2+6)+14(1+2)+7(1+3)$ (Commutative Property of Addition and Distributive Property)

F3: $8(2x+3)+7(2y+3)+15(z+4)$ (Commutative Property of Addition and Distributive Property)

F4: $11(4g+1)+30(3f+1)+12(6h+1)$ (Commutative Property of Addition and Distributive Property)

F5: $7(90-3)+2\times 129+4\times 99$ (Distributive Property)

F6: $9(140+1)+(10+2)(140-1)+25\times 38$ (Distributive Property)

G3: $8\times 30+3\times 140+2\times 30$ (Distributive Property)

G4: 260×3 (Combining Like Terms and Associative Property of Addition)

G5: 150×3 (Combining Like Terms and Associative Property of Addition)

G6: 100×3 (Combining Like Terms and Associative Property of Addition)

H3: $5(5x+7y+17z+14)$ (Distributive Property)

H4: $6(13+10x+11y+z)$ (Distributive Property)

H5: $8(80+1)+9(90+1)+7(80-1)$ (Distributive Property)

H6: $4(200+1)+5(300+1)+6(400+1)$ (Distributive Property)

Extend Your Thinking

1. Answers will vary.
2. Answers will vary.

Lesson 3.2 Practice: Practice With Equivalent Expressions

1. a. Answers may vary. The best way to simplify it is $3x+2y+400$; b. $2,500; c. $3x+2y-5z+400$; d. $60
2. a. $40s+20t-100$; b. $20(2s+t-5)$; c. $36s+18t-100$; d. 14 pairs of shoes and 21 shirts (answers may vary)

Extend Your Thinking

1. Answers will vary.

Lesson 3.2 Common Core Assessment Practice

1. b
2. a
3. c
4. a
5. c

Lesson 3.3 Activity: Secret Codes With Equivalent Expressions

Answers will vary.

Extend Your Thinking

1. Answers will vary.
2. Answers will vary.
3. Answers will vary.

Lesson 3.3 Code Creator Handout

Answers will vary.

Lesson 3.3 Journal Log

Answers will vary.

Lesson 3.3 Practice: Working With Equivalent Expressions

1. a. Commutative property; b. Answers will vary. Students will most likely notice that Jessica can combine $9b$ and $15b$ using the associative property to group similar variables. They will rewrite the expression as $24b - 12c$; c. No. Jessica should have noticed that the GCF that both coefficients share is 12 and factored a 12 out using the distributive property. Her final expression should have been $12(2b - c)$; d. Answers will vary. Students need to point out that the variables b and c both represent different numbers. Students can also point out that each coefficient simply represents how many of variable *b* and variable *c* are in the problem. You cannot combine the two variables because it misrepresents the value. Students might give examples, such as if you subtract 15 from 20 you get 5. Rewriting this as products of 5, the problem looks like this: $4(5) - 3(5) = 1(5)$. However, if you subtract 18 from 20 and get 2, it wouldn't work the same because both numbers cannot be written as a product of the same numbers. $4(5) - 2(9)$ does not equal 2(5) or 2(9). It works the same way for variables.
2. a. $24b + 36g$; b. $12(2b + 3g)$; c. 84; 3 times 20 is 60 plus 2 times 12 is 24. 60 plus 24 is 84; d. $1,008

Extend Your Thinking

1. Answers will vary.

Lesson 3.3 Common Core Assessment Practice

1. d
2. b
3. a
4. d
5. c

Lesson 3.4 Activity: Fantasy Football Expressions

Answers will vary.

Extend Your Thinking

1. Answers will vary.
2. Answers will vary.

Lesson 3.4 Draft Board Handout

Answers will vary.

Quarterbacks					
	Completions	**Yards**	**Touchdowns**	**Interceptions**	**Points**
1. Drew Brees					
2014	456	4,952	33	17	392
2013	446	5,162	39	12	436
Avg.	451	4,877	36	14.5	414
2. Ben Roethlisberger					
2014	408	4,952	32	9	399
2013	375	4,261	28	14	335
Avg.	391.5	4,606.5	30	12.5	367
3. Andrew Luck					
2014	380	4,761	40	16	404
2013	343	3,822	23	9	299
Avg.	361.5	4,291.5	31.5	12.5	351.5
4. Peyton Manning					
2014	395	4,727	39	15	402
2013	450	5,477	55	10	519
Avg.	422.5	5,102	47	12.5	460.5
5. Matt Ryan					
2014	415	4,694	28	14	361
2013	439	4,515	26	17	340
Avg.	427	4,604.5	27	15.5	350.5
6. Eli Manning					
2014	379	4,410	30	14	351
2013	317	3,818	18	27	261
Avg.	348	4,114	24	20.5	306
7. Aaron Rodgers					
2014	341	4,381	38	5	395
2012	371	4,295	39	8	392
Avg.	356	4,338	38.5	6.5	393.5
8. Philip Rivers					
2014	379	4,286	31	18	340
2013	378	4,478	32	11	368
Avg.	378.5	4,382	31.5	14.5	354

Quarterbacks	Completions	Yards	Touchdowns	Interceptions	Points
9. Matthew Stafford					
2014	363	4,257	22	12	313
2013	446	4,650	29	19	348
Avg.	404.5	4,454	25.5	15.5	330.5
10. Tom Brady					
2014	373	4,109	33	9	356
2013	380	4,343	25	11	333
Avg.	376.5	4,226	29	10	344.5
11. Russell Wilson					
2014	285	3,475	20	7	269
2013	257	3,357	26	9	280
Avg.	271	3,416	23	8	274.5

Running Backs	Attempts	Yards	Touchdowns	Points
1. DeMarco Murray				
2014	392	1,845	13	302
2013	217	1,121	9	188
Avg.	304.5	1,483	11	245
2. Le'Veon Bell				
2014	290	1,361	8	213
2013	244	890	8	161
Avg.	267	1,125.5	8	187
3. LeSean McCoy				
2014	312	1,319	5	193
2013	314	1,607	9	246
Avg.	313	1,463	7	219.5
4. Marshawn Lynch				
2014	280	1,306	13	237
2013	301	1,257	12	228
Avg.	290.5	1,281.5	12.5	232.5
5. Arian Foster				
2014	260	1,246	8	199
2012	351	1,424	15	267
Avg.	305.5	1,335	11.5	233
6. Eddie Lacy				
2014	246	1,124	9	191
2013	284	1,178	11	212
Avg.	265	1,151	10	201.5

Running Backs	Attempts	Yards	Touchdowns	Points
7. Alfred Morris				
2014	265	1,074	8	182
2013	276	1,275	7	198
Avg.	270.5	1,174.5	7.5	190
8. Matt Forte				
2014	266	1,038	6	167
2013	289	1,339	9	217
Avg.	277.5	1,188.5	7.5	192
9. Jamaal Charles				
2014	206	1,033	9	178
2013	259	1,287	12	227
Avg.	232.5	1,160	10.5	202.5
10. Frank Gore				
2014	255	1,106	4	161
2013	276	1,128	9	195
Avg.	265.5	1,117	6.5	178

Wide Receivers	Receptions	Yards	Touchdowns	Points
1. Antonio Brown				
2014	129	1,698	13	261
2013	110	1,499	8	209
Avg.	119.5	1,598.5	10.5	235
2. Demaryius Thomas				
2014	111	1,619	11	239
2013	92	1,430	14	236
Avg.	101.5	1,524.5	12.5	237.5
3. Julio Jones				
2014	104	1,593	6	205
2012	79	1,198	10	188
Avg.	91.5	1,395.5	8	196.5
4. Jordy Nelson				
2014	98	1,519	13	240
2013	85	1,314	8	188
Avg.	91.5	1,416.5	10.5	214
5. Emmanuel Sanders				
2014	101	1,404	9	204
2013	67	740	6	117
Avg.	84	1,072	7.5	160.5

Wide Receivers	Receptions	Yards	Touchdowns	Points
6. T.Y. Hilton				
2014	82	1,345	7	185
2013	82	1,083	5	146
Avg.	82	1,214	6	165.5
7. Dez Bryant				
2014	88	1,320	16	237
2013	93	1,233	13	210
Avg.	90.5	1,276.5	14.5	223.5
8. Jeremy Maclin				
2014	85	1,318	10	201
2012	69	857	7	135
Avg.	77	1,087.5	8.5	168
9. Alshon Jeffery				
2014	85	1,133	10	182
2013	89	1,421	7	193
Avg.	87	1,277	8.5	187.5
10. Calvin Johnson				
2014	71	1,077	8	163
2013	84	1,492	12	229
Avg.	77.5	1,284.5	10	196

Lesson 3.4 Fantasy Point Calculations

1. a. Answers will vary based on players selected; b. Answers will vary; c. There may be a variety of answers, but the correct answer should be in the form $16x = y$, where y represents the statistical average of the 2 years and x represents the per-game average.
2. a. Answers will vary based on players selected; b. Answers will vary; c. There may be a variety of answers, but the correct answer should be in the form $16x = y$, where y represents the statistical average of the 2 years and x represents the per-game average.
3. a. Answers will vary based on players selected; b. Answers will vary; c. There may be a variety of answers, but all answers should be in the form $16x = y$, where y represents the statistical average of the 2 years and x represents the per-game average.

Lesson 3.4 Fantasy Football Simulated Game

Answers will vary.

Lesson 3.4 Practice: Solving Equations

1. a. Week 1: $804, Week 2: $882, Week 3: $729, Week 4: $755; b. Answers will vary. Students might explain that they can use the average of the first 4 weeks to determine a best guess for the profits for each week that the store is open; c. $792.5x$; the average profit over the first 4 weeks is $792.5. Students might argue that they can round it up to $793, in which case

the expression would be $793x$; d. \$41,210 or \$41,236; e. Answers will vary. Students should make the connection that x represents the number of weeks that the store is operating. They might explain that Sergio cannot just subtract the 350 cost once but has to subtract it every week, thus is needs to be included as a coefficient of the variable x because the cost to run the store has to be extended over the number of weeks of operation.

2. a. $2s-500$; b. 15 snacks: \$470 loss, 50 snacks: \$400 loss, 300 snacks: \$100 profit; c. Nedal needs to sell 250 snacks. Students should notice that it costs \$500 to purchase a snack machine, so he has to sell enough snacks to at least earn back his \$500 and break even. If each snack is \$2, then he has to sell 250 snacks to earn \$500; d. $10s-2500$. The expression to find the net earnings from one machine is $2s-500$. Because each machine sells the same number of snacks and she has five machines, you can multiply the expression for one machine by five to represent her total earnings; e. Students should recognize that both terms have a common factor of 5 and can factor it out using the distributive property and can write the expression $5(2s-500)$.

Extend Your Thinking

1. Answers will vary.

Lesson 3.4 Common Core Assessment Practice

1. b
2. c
3. d
4. a
5. d

Lesson 3.5 Activity: Inequalities in Our Lives

Answers will vary.

Extend Your Thinking

1. Answers will vary.
2. Answers will vary.

Lesson 3.5 Practice: Working With Inequalities

1. a. $r \geq 50$; b. $2c+15 \geq 50$, $c \geq 18$; c. $50 \leq r < 150$; d. Because you are trying to find the maximum, that means Adeline has only raised the minimum amount of money possible to earn a spot on the field trip. Because the lowest multiple of 7 that would earn a spot on the trip is \$56, you have to assume that is the amount she has already raised. Thus the inequality would be $7j+56 \geq 150$. Solving for the inequality shows that $j \geq 14$. *Note.* It is greater than or equal to because anything less than 150 does not qualify, which means that raising \$150 exactly would earn Adeline a spot in the drawing.
2. a. $t < 21.5$ minutes; b. $f-2(30) \leq 32$. The maximum temperature is 92 degrees Fahrenheit.

Extend Your Thinking

1. Answers will vary.

Lesson 3.5 Common Core Assessment Practice

1. a
2. c
3. d
4. c
5. b; She still has 12 full sets remaining plus the set that she is currently finishing.

Lesson 3.6 Activity: Variables in Flight

1–8. Answers will vary based on student selections.

9. Answers will vary, but students may point out that the weather or current wind speed may affect the flight time. Some students may also point to traffic at a certain airport that might make flights have to enter into hold patterns or slightly alter their routes to arrive a bit later.

Extend Your Thinking

1. Answers will vary. Students will probably notice that the larger flights tend to have a higher average rate of speed. Students may also notice a difference in the speeds of different manufacturers.
2. Students should notice that tailwinds will shorten the flight times while a headwind will increase the flight time.

Lesson 3.6 Flight Tracking Worksheet

1–5. Answers will vary.

Lesson 3.6 Practice: Working With Independent and Dependent Variables

1. a. $45t = d$;

   b. Answers are in bold:

Time (minutes)	Distance (miles)
30 minutes	**22.5 miles**
60 minutes	**45 miles**
120 minutes	**90 miles**
150 minutes	**112.50 miles**
240 minutes	**180 miles**
255 minutes	**191.25 miles**

   c. 105 miles. Students should subtract the 20 minute stop from the total time to calculate the distance; d. 3 hours and 32 minutes

2. a. $80t = o$, $800r = o$

   b. Answers are in bold:

Rows	Oranges
3 rows	**2,400 oranges**
6 rows	**4,800 oranges**
8 rows	**6,400 oranges**
10.5 rows	**8,400 oranges**
12 rows	**9,600 oranges**
20 rows	**16,000 oranges**

c. $17,050; d. 82% (rounded to the nearest percent)

Extend Your Thinking

1. Answers may vary. Even though one of the ratios is comparing distance and the other is comparing speed, the two ratios are equivalent. This shows that the unit rate of 1.151 nautical miles to 1 mile is constant regardless of what is being measured. With all else being equal, the ratio of nautical miles to miles will always be consistent.

Lesson 3.6 Common Core Assessment Practice

1. b
2. d
3. c
4. c
5. b

SECTION IV: GEOMETRY

Lesson 4.1 Activity: Creating Shapes on a Coordinate Grid

Answers will vary based on cards used.

Extend Your Thinking

1. Answers will vary.
2. Answers will vary.

Lesson 4.1 Index Cards

Answers are in bold:

Level 1 Find the area of a rectangle with vertices at (-4, 5), (-4, 7), (2, 5), and (2,7). **12**	Level 1 Find the area of a triangle with vertices at (7, 2), (4, 2), and (4, -3). **7.5**
Level 1 Create a rectangle with a base from points (4, 6) and (8, 6) and an area of 4. **Answers will vary; (4, 7) (8, 7)**	Level 1 Create a triangle with a base from points (1, 1) to (-3, 1) and an area of 8. **Answers will vary; (-3, 5)**
Level 2 Create a trapezoid with an area of 6 and one base from (-4,1) to (-1, 1). **Answers will vary; (-3, 4) (-2, 4)**	Level 2 Create a parallelogram with an area of 4 and a base from (1, -3) to (5, -3). **Answers will vary; (2, -2) (6, -2)**

Level 2 Create a triangle in Quadrant III with an area of 3. **Answers will vary; (-4, -1) (-1, -1) (-1, -3)**	Level 2 Create a rectangle in Quadrant II with an area of 6. **Answers will vary; (-5, 4) (-2, 4) (-5, 6) (-2, 6)**
Level 2 Create a triangle with an area of 4 that has one vertex at (-4, -4). **Answers will vary; (-4, 0) (-2, 0)**	Level 2 Create a triangle with an area of 4.5 that has one vertex at (3, -6). **Answers will vary; (3, -3) (6, -3)**

Lesson 4.1 Practice: Geometry on the Coordinate Plane

1. a. (-9, 8); b. 210 square yards; c. (9, -7)
2. a. (7, 6) and (10, 3); b. Answers will vary. One example of two points is (-1, 3) and (-6, 6).

Extend Your Thinking

1. Answers will vary.

Lesson 4.1 Common Core Assessment Practice

1. b
2. a
3. c
4. a
5. d

Lesson 4.2 Activity: Volume in a Vacuum

1–5. Answers will vary.

Extend Your Thinking

1. Answers will vary.
2. Answers will vary.

Lesson 4.2 Volume of the Ship Worksheet

1. Answers will vary.
2. Answers will vary.
3. Answers will vary.

Lesson 4.2 Practice: Working With Volume

1. a. 96 inches cubed; b. 12,000 cubic feet; c. 1,500 cubic feet. Because the dimensions of the actual replica are 40 feet, 20 feet, and 15 feet, the dimensions of the company's cabin would be 20 feet, 10 feet, and 7.5 feet after being reduced by a factor of one half. Multiplying them together gets 1,500 cubic feet; d. $\frac{1}{8}$; e. Answers will vary. Students may notice that the ratio of volumes is the cube of the scale factor and relate that to the three dimensions taken into account when calculating the volume.

2. a. 96 cubic feet; b. 76.8 cubic feet; c. 6.4 hours. By dividing the total volume that needs to be filled by the amount of water that Caleb can fill in a minute, students will find that it will take him 384 minutes. Convert this to hours by dividing the minutes by 60 to get 6.4 hours.

Extend Your Thinking

1. Answers will vary. This is more of an open-ended question designed to get the students to think about the relationship with numbers and volume. Students may believe that the basic capsule looks similar to a cone. The formula for volume of a cone is $V = (\pi r^2 h)/3$. Students do not need to calculate the actual volume of the ships; they are simply looking for a proportional relationship between the two volumes and what the corresponding scale factor is between the two ships. For example, the difference between the volume of the Mercury craft and the Gemini craft is 0.85 cubic meters. This translates to a percent increase of about 1.85 cubic meters. Students should experiment with fractional scale factors to see if they can get close to the 1.85 cubic meter difference. Students might get pretty close by multiplying each dimension by $\frac{6}{5}$. Students should realize that the scale factors for each dimension of an object will have the effect of increasing or decreasing the volume by the cube of the scale factor because of the three dimensions.

Lesson 4.2 Common Core Assessment Practice

1. d
2. b
3. c
4. a
5. c

Lesson 4.3 Activity: Nothing but Nets

1. Net 1: Polyhedron 3; Net 2: Polyhedron 2; Net 3: Polyhedron 4; Net 4: Polyhedron 5; Net 5: Polyhedron 1
2. Answers will vary based on the base card selected.
3. Students should generalize the formula $6s^2$ for the surface area of a cube. Students should generalize the formula $2lw + 2lh + 2wh$ for the surface area of the rectangular prism.
4. Answers will vary, based on the scale factor chosen.
5. Students should notice that the relationship between the increase in the scale factor increases the surface area of the rectangular prism and cube by the scale factor squared.
6. Answers will vary.

Extend Your Thinking

1. Answers will vary. Student should notice that an increase by a fractional scale factor will decrease the surface area of the object by the square of the fractional scale factor.
2. Answers will vary. Generally, fractional scale factors will decrease the surface area, and the whole number scale factors will increase it.

Lesson 4.3 Sample Base Cards and Scaled Factor Slips

Answers are in bold:

<table>
<tr><td>Cube
Side Length: 4 cm</td><td>Rectangular Prism
Length: 2 cm
Width: 3 cm
Height: 4 cm</td><td>Cube
Side Length: 5 in</td><td>Rectangular Prism
Length: 6 in
Width: 2 in
Height: 5 in</td></tr>
<tr><td colspan="2">Surface Area (Cube): 96 cm²
Surface Area (Rect. Prism): 52 cm²</td><td colspan="2">Surface Area (Cube): 150 in²
Surface Area (Rect. Prism): 104 in²</td></tr>
<tr><td>Cube
Side Length: 2 ft</td><td>Rectangular Prism
Length: 8 ft
Width: 5 ft
Height: 2 ft</td><td>Cube
Side Length: 6 m</td><td>Rectangular Prism
Length: 4 m
Width: 1 m
Height: 10 m</td></tr>
<tr><td colspan="2">Surface Area (Cube): 24 ft²
Surface Area (Rect. Prism): 132 ft²</td><td colspan="2">Surface Area (Cube): 216 m²
Surface Area (Rect. Prism): 108 m²</td></tr>
</table>

Lesson 4.3 Surface Area Calculation Worksheet

1–3. Answers will vary.

4. Students should notice that the surface area of an object will increase by the square of the scale factor because both dimensions are being increased by that scale factor.
5. Students will find that multiplying the surface area by the square of the scale factor will work.

Lesson 4.3 Practice: Surface Area and Nets

1. a. Answers will vary; b. 9 cm squared should be written in each face; c. $A = 6s^2$
2. a. Answers will vary. Students might determine a base of 4 meters, a width of 10 meters, and a height of 5 meters; b. 880 meters squared; c. Answers will vary. The scale factor of the area was increased by a factor of 4. Because both dimensions were increased by a factor of 2 and area involves multiplying the dimensions together, the scale factor increase for the area will be the square of the scale factor increase for the dimensions.

Extend Your Thinking

1. The dimensions of the three pyramids are: largest (base of 230 m and slant height of 186 m), middle (base of 216 m and height of 179 m), and smallest (base of 109 m and slant height of 86 m). Surface area of the largest is 138,460 square meters, surface area of the middle is 123,984 square meters, and surface area of smallest is 30,629 square meters.

Lesson 4.3 Common Core Assessment Practice

1. b
2. c
3. a
4. d
5. a

SECTION V: STATISTICS AND PROBABILITY

Lesson 5.1 Activity: A Discussion of Data

Answers will vary based on the questions used.

Extend Your Thinking

1. Answers will vary.
2. Answers will vary.

Lesson 5.1 Data Observations Worksheet

Part I

1. At this point, students should start to see the numbers growing around a certain area. They can make that observation and write down a measure of center based on where the data is accumulating.
2. Students should notice a pattern and write down a measure of center based on the data. Students should be able to think about the question that they asked and explain why they think the data is falling around that set of numbers. They can defend their answer by what they know about the question that they asked.
3. This question requires the students to recognize the real-world applications of their question. They will notice the measure of variation and be able to explain why it would most likely fall within this range. For example, if students are asking questions regarding the number of siblings that each student in the class has, the measure of variation will never get very large due to the reality of the number of kids a family can reasonably support.

Part II

1. Students will either notice the numbers staying the same or the numbers shifting toward a different measure of center.
2. If the measure of center shifted, the students can point to the small sample size of students not being as accurate as a larger size; if the measure of center stayed relatively similar, students can make the observation that most people in a peer group will share similar interests/experiences. They might also be able to defend the statement that even a smaller sample size of data can give a decent picture of a group of people.
3. Students will probably begin to agree that the larger the number of data items, the more accurate the data.

Part III

1. Students can look at the data and notice where most of the numbers are falling. They can then make a best guess of where the measures of center might fall.
2. Depending on the question asked, the range of data values might be different. Students can relate the data values to what they know is realistic about the question they are asking. Examples will be a wide range.
3. Depending on the statistical question, students might realize that outliers can affect a set of data in a misleading way, an overly negative way, or an overly positive way. If most students score well on a test but one student scores a really low score, that might influence more of a negative perception of the success of the assessment.

4. Students will argue that outliers can be misleading and should thus be ignored as not being an accurate representation of the statistical question asked. Other students might argue that an outlier, while not as important, should not simply be ignored because they do represent certain situations that need to be accounted for. Students might also make the connection that one item that is an outlier in one data set might turn into more of a trend depending on changes in the situation.

Lesson 5.1 Practice: Analyzing Data

1. a. 85.25; b. 94; c. 89
2. a. Answers will vary. This is not a statistical question because it yields only a single answer and has no variation with which to compare it; b. Answers will vary. Example: How many different states has each student in the class visited?; c. Answers will vary. Example: Students will probably figure that most students have visited the states that border their own state, so you may have answers ranging from 1–5 or so depending on the geographic location of the school. A student who has traveled to more states might assume that other students have as well and list a higher range of numbers; d. Answers will vary.

Extend Your Thinking

1. Answers will vary.
2. Answers will vary.

Lesson 5.1 Common Core Assessment Practice

1. c
2. b
3. d
4. c
5. b

Lesson 5.2 Activity: Defending a Data Set

1. Answers will vary.
2. Data Set 1: Mean: 84.8, Median: 85, Mode: 83, and Range: 11; Data Set 2: Mean: 505.1, Median: 550.5, Mode: 563, and Range: 820; Data Set 3: Mean: 2.25, Median: 2, Mode: 2, and Range: 6
3. The mean is the best for Data Set 2, the median is the best for Data Set 1, and the mode is the best for Data Set 3. In Data Set 1, most of the numbers are clustered around a specific number, so the median is the best. In Data Set 2, the numbers are more spread out, so it would be more useful to find the arithmetic average of these numbers. In Data Set 3, 2 siblings appears an overwhelming number of times, so this set of data can be accurately represented by the mode.
4. Answers will vary.
5. Answers will vary.
6. Data Set 1: Mode: 83, Median: 84.5, and Mean: 83; Data Set 2: Mode: 563, Median: 549, and Mean: 483.2; Data Set 3: Mode: 2, Median: 2, Mean: 2.6

7. Students should notice that the mean of the numbers is most greatly affected by an outlier. This is because the mean takes into account the value of each individual number in the set much more so than the other two measures of center do.

Extend Your Thinking

1. Answers will vary. Students should notice the difference between the highest and lowest numbers in the set when compared with the mean. Students might notice that if the highest number is further away from the mean, then the mean will decrease when both numbers are removed. If the lowest number is further away from the mean, then the mean will increase when both numbers are removed.

Lesson 5.2 Graphing Data

1. Data Set 3 (although it can vary). Students might argue that the dot plot will most easily show Data Set 3 because it best shows the frequency of one number.
2. Data Set 2. A histogram works best because it displays a range of data that works well for a larger range of numbers, which you see in Data Set 2.
3. Data Set 1. The box plot will best show the scores for the test because it shows very clearly the median, highest value, and lowest value as well as breaks the data up into quartiles, which allows for easy analysis of test scores.

Lesson 5.2 Defending a Data Set Worksheet

1. The mean would be the best measure of center for Data Set 2.
2. The median would be the best measure of center for Data Set 1.
3. The mode would be the best measure of center for Data Set 3.
4. Students will most likely choose Data Set 2 for the mean (although answers may vary) and point to the fact that the mean will best represent the wide range of miles traveled better than any other measure of center.
5. Students will most likely choose Data Set 1 for the median because all of the test scores are very consistent, and the median would accurately represent this. The median would also not be as affected by the outlier, which might give a lower representation of the test scores.
6. The mode is the best way to represent Data Set 3 because it shows which one occurs the most in the data set, which is an accurate way to represent the number of siblings a student has.
7. a. Generally the mean is a good measure of center for a wide range of data items, especially if you want to take into account each of the data items in the set. For example, if a trucking company is tracking the mileage for each driver, it will not want to discount a number that is much higher or lower than the usual mileage, so it would use the mean; b. The median is a good measure of center when most of the data items are clustered pretty closely together; c. The mode is a good measure of center when one or two of the items are appearing at a much higher number than the others. The mode is especially useful if you really are only worried about which item is most common. For example, if an airline company is trying to see how many bags are checked by its customers, the company might not be as worried about the mean or median because the mode would give it a good number on which to proceed with future plans.

8. Students will probably notice that outliers do not usually affect the mode and median whereas the mean can be greatly affected by an outlier depending on the number of data items in the data set.

Lesson 5.2 Practice: Analyzing Sets of Data

1. a.

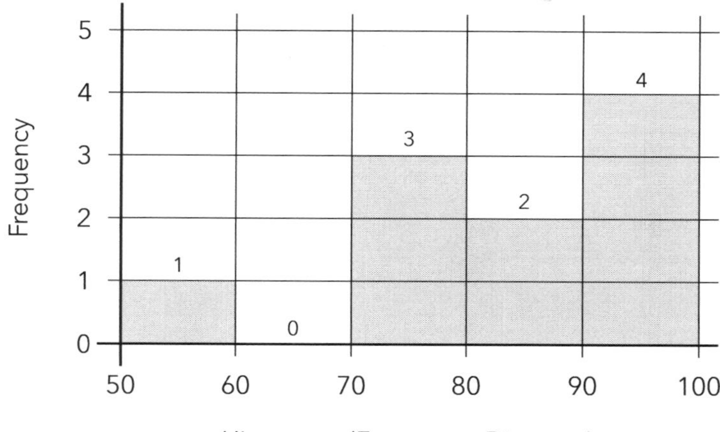

Mrs. Carmichael's Fourth-Grade Test Scores

   b. mean: 83.7, median: 86.5, mode: no mode, range: 42; c. 56. Answers will vary; d. 85.4; e. Answers will vary.

Extend Your Thinking

1. Answers will vary.

Lesson 5.2 Common Core Assessment Practice

1. a
2. c
3. c
4. d
5. a

ABOUT THE AUTHOR

James M. Moroney teaches sixth-grade math, Algebra I honors, and geometry honors at Our Lady of Mercy Catholic School in Louisiana, where he lives with his wife, Joan, and son, Connor. He is a graduate of the gifted program at McKinley Senior High School. He attended Louisiana State University, where he earned his bachelor of arts in English with a concentration in secondary education. He is secondary certified in both English and mathematics.

COMMON CORE STATE STANDARDS ALIGNMENT

Lesson	Common Core State Standards
Lesson 1.1	6.RP.A Understand ratio concepts and use ratio reasoning to solve problems.
Lesson 1.2	6.RP.A Understand ratio concepts and use ratio reasoning to solve problems.
Lesson 1.3	6.RP.A Understand ratio concepts and use ratio reasoning to solve problems.
Lesson 1.3	6.RP.A Understand ratio concepts and use ratio reasoning to solve problems.
Lesson 2.1	6.NS.A Apply and extend previous understandings of multiplication and division to divide fractions by fractions.
Lesson 2.2	6.NS.B Compute fluently with multi-digit numbers and find common factors and multiples.
Lesson 2.3	6.NS.C Apply and extend previous understandings of numbers to the system of rational numbers.
Lesson 2.4	6.NS.C Apply and extend previous understandings of numbers to the system of rational numbers.
Lesson 2.5	6.NS.C Apply and extend previous understandings of numbers to the system of rational numbers.
Lesson 3.1	6.EE.A Apply and extend previous understandings of arithmetic to algebraic expressions.
Lesson 3.2	6.EE.A Apply and extend previous understandings of arithmetic to algebraic expressions.
Lesson 3.3	6.EE.A Apply and extend previous understandings of arithmetic to algebraic expressions.
Lesson 3.4	6.EE.B Reason about and solve one-variable equations and inequalities.
Lesson 3.5	6.EE.B Reason about and solve one-variable equations and inequalities.
Lesson 3.6	6.EE.B Reason about and solve one-variable equations and inequalities.

Lesson	Common Core State Standards
Lesson 4.1	6.G.A Solve real-world and mathematical problems involving area, surface area, and volume.
Lesson 4.2	6.G.A Solve real-world and mathematical problems involving area, surface area, and volume.
Lesson 4.3	6.G.A Solve real-world and mathematical problems involving area, surface area, and volume.
Lesson 5.1	6.SP.A Develop understanding of statistical variability.
Lesson 5.2	6.SP.B Summarize and describe distributions.